THE LAW AND
THE COMMONWEALTH

THE LAW AND
THE COMMONWEALTH

BY

R. T. E. LATHAM

GREENWOOD PRESS, PUBLISHERS
WESTPORT, CONNECTICUT

Originally published in 1937 as an essay in
Survey of British Commonwealth Affairs
(W. K. Hancock) and in 1949 as a separate monograph by
Oxford University Press, London

Reprinted with the permission
of Oxford University Press

First Greenwood Reprinting 1970

Library of Congress Catalogue Card Number 70-104250

SBN 8371-3974-0

Printed in the United States of America

INTRODUCTION

THIS essay was first published in 1937 as a lawyer's contribution to my *Survey of British Commonwealth Affairs*. There are compelling reasons for re-issuing it in its own covers. Admittedly, there has accumulated since 1937 a good deal of new constitutional data, which the author, if he were still alive, would have wished to discuss in a revised edition of his work; but his work in its original form contains so much fundamental thought that it will not, in this generation at least, grow out of date. To a layman like myself it offers invaluable guidance amidst those intricate constitutional issues which 'the autonomous nations of the Commonwealth' debated with each other so intently between the two great wars of this century. To the lawyer it offers a great deal more. Simple Austinianism, with its psychological view of law as a command and its requirement of a determinate sovereign, seems nowadays very remote from the juristic complexities of the British Commonwealth, in which so many systems of law co-exist, each analysable as an entity in itself, but each also in some way bound to all the others and to the whole. This essay calls in Kelsen's Pure Theory of Law to illuminate these complexities. Jurists may possibly differ among themselves about the precise contribution to the essay's merits made by 'that agile little creature the *grundnorm*' (I am now quoting Latham's own talk); but they will all agree that the sound learning and penetrating analysis contained in the essay ought no longer to be left hidden at the back of another man's book. Latham's work now appears under its own title and in its own right.

Appearing thus, it will commemorate not only a brilliant scholar but a brave airman, Flying-Officer Richard Thomas Edwin Latham, a man of subtle mind who believed in simple truths and gave his life, as he had lived it, affirming and upholding those truths. He was an Australian Rhodes Scholar, a Fellow of All Souls, a Lecturer at King's College, London, a practising barrister, a brilliant academic lawyer, a young man already marked out for the highest achievement. When he wrote his exposition of the legal order of the Commonwealth he was only 27 years old; when the war broke out he was only 30. For his special gifts and training the Foreign Office work to which he was called in 1939 would have given ample opportunities of service throughout the war. But he preferred a more direct and dangerous service and participation in the common experience of his own generation of young men. He volunteered for the Royal Air Force, was called up in 1941, went to Canada for his training, and graduated as Leading Aircraftsman. In England he was commissioned as Observer. His last flight was over the Norwegian coast, on 15 August 1943, when his aircraft and its crew were reported missing. For a time his friends hoped that he might still be living, perhaps as a prisoner; but on 11 April 1944 the Air Ministry notified him as killed on active service.

There was in him a deeply planted consistency which steadily revealed and fulfilled itself throughout his thirty-four years of life. From a friend who was his contemporary at Scotch College, Melbourne, at the University of Melbourne, and later at Oxford, I have learnt something of the steadfastness with which from boyhood into manhood he pursued the two-fold adventure of ideas and of the common experience of life. From the latter he was at first somewhat shut off by an illness of childhood. He went to school late, and with a complete lack of aptitude for athletic sports: in consequence, his successes were chiefly in class, or in the more intellectual activities of school society. 'He was quite well liked by most people,' his friend writes, 'very much admired by some, and in a small circle greatly loved. That was true of him throughout, I think.' But at Melbourne University the circle of his intimate friends grew larger, and when people spoke of him they used his Christian name; he had become Dick Latham, or Dick. At the University he found also enlarged opportunities for social activity and leadership. He was elected president of the Students' Representative Council. Moreover, it was then that he first revealed his zest 'to go exploring in some discomfort to see what the world was like'. He explored the New Hebrides and New Caledonia in order to study the working of a condominium and to see how the French governed colonial peoples; just as some years later he travelled impecuniously from Melbourne to Oxford by way of Japan and right across Soviet Russia, in order to see for himself something of the Soviet experiment.

In 1931 he went with his Rhodes Scholarship to Magdalen; in 1933 he took his First in the Honours School of Jurisprudence; in 1934 he was elected to All Souls. We have now in our Common Room some of the books—the poetry, essays, and novels—which he had bought for his own pleasure. His Oxford days were for him a time of blossoming in the love of literature and music and in the enjoyment of friendship. There too he mastered the academic disciplines which he employed so powerfully in expounding the legal structure of the Commonwealth and in the other learned writings which are listed at the end of this book. He could easily have made himself a professional philosopher or historian; but the philosophical and historical study of English law was his natural inheritance from his father, the present Chief Justice of the Commonwealth of Australia. He taught law at Oxford, he taught and practised it in London, he took an active part in Chatham House studies, and attended the Toronto Conference on British Commonwealth Relations. All this might have been expected from a man with such a marked record of intellectual achievement. But all the time he was still pursuing—with a purpose which now was sharply focused—that other adventure in the common experience of life. It took him to Republican Spain, to drive a lorry for one of the relief societies on the Bordeaux–Barcelona route. His friends thought him an incompetent driver; if they were right, he must have taken his life in his hands many times on the Pyrenean passes. At that time the *Luftwaffe* was getting professional practice in Spain; and perhaps it was then that Dick Latham decided that he would one day make his own personal answer in the R.A.F. to Nazi bullying. In retrospect, his decision seems inevitable: for it was the same brutal abuse of power which threatened both the freedom of intellectual life and the decencies of common life. He believed in both. In defence of both he offered not only his intellect—for him that was not enough—but himself.

W. K. HANCOCK

ALL SOULS COLLEGE,
    July, 1948

TABLE OF CONTENTS

THE LAW AND
THE COMMONWEALTH

By R. T. E. LATHAM

THE LAW AND THE COMMONWEALTH

By R. T. E. LATHAM

I

THE COMMON LAW, ITS NATURE AND EXPANSION

'SIXTHLY', wrote Sir Edward Coke, in a peroration to his report of a great case, 'it appeareth, that the jurisprudence of the Common Law of England is a science sociable and copious: sociable, in that it agreeth with the principles and rules of other excellent sciences, divine and human, copious, for that . . . there should be such a multitude and *farrago* of authorities in all successions of ages, in our books and bookcases, for the deciding of the point of so rare an accident.'[1] This essay is in large measure a study in the sociability and the copiousness of the Common Law in a particular field. The author of this dictum personified the pride of the Common Law in its own integrity and all-sufficiency, in an age when it was still fighting its rivals.[2] That arrogance of the Common Law persists in England to the present day in the unbroken tradition of the courts. For the most part it is a self-regard which coincides comfortably with the neat, logical self-regard of analytical jurisprudence, fortifying analytical theory with the flesh and blood of a living institution. Theory requires that formally the law should never be at a loss for an answer.[3] In practice, says Coke, the Common Law of England never is at a loss for an answer, and that a good one. Jurists may say that law rests on compulsion, but the English judge, taking it for granted that his order will be executed, needs no *fasces*: for him, his robes, which link him directly with Coke and all other lusty English judges, are authority enough.

Other intolerances of the Common Law accord less well with theory. A notable instance is its treatment of statutes. Abandoning the medieval idea that there was a fundamental or immutable law,[4]

---

[1] *Calvin's Case* (1608) 7 Co. Rep. 1a, 28a.

[2] It was actually defeated shortly afterwards by its rival, Equity, but Equity rapidly assumed the character and texture of the Common Law, and the Courts of Equity and Common Law were amalgamated in the nineteenth century. In this chapter, unless otherwise indicated, when the Common Law is spoken of Equity is included, but not statute law.

[3] See, e.g., the controversy in international law, whether there can be a 'non-justiciable dispute', discussed in Lauterpacht, *The Function of Law in the International Community*.

[4] As expressed in, e.g., *Bonham's Case* (1610) 8 Co. Rep. 114.

the Common Law recognized the legislative supremacy of Parliament.[1] But to the words of the Parliament whose literal authority it thus recognized it accorded none of that aura of respect and generosity of interpretation with which it surrounded its own doctrines. The courts never entered into the spirit of the Benthamite game, but treated the statute throughout as an interloper upon the rounded majesty of the Common Law. The tendency still persists: the courts show a ripe appreciation of institutions of long standing, whether founded by statute or in the Common Law, but they inhibit themselves from seizing the spirit of institutions and situations which are in substance the creation of modern legislation.[2]

Of international law the Common Law is still less patient: it exists in the English courts only as a presumption to be followed in the absence of a clear rule of municipal law.[3] Further, the Common Law now grows wholly from within. Its last spontaneous 'reception' of a body of alien doctrine was the reception of mercantile law in the eighteenth century.

In short, the modern Common Law has ceased to be 'sociable'. It is impatient of other kinds and systems of law, and does not eagerly claim kinship with moral science or natural reason. Coke justified the Common Law as a system closely conformable to the Law of Nature;[4] his modern successors find the Common Law self-justified. This is not vanity, for popular esteem combines with judicial tradition to give the courts a rare institutional strength. The Common Law is *par excellence* the law of the courts, and its courts have a unique majesty. In the United States, where no parliament has been set over against them as strong after its fashion as they in theirs, the judges have been driven by the traditions of their craft to establish a conscientious judicial tyranny.

This, then, is the nature and quality of the law which has extended itself, in one form or another, over one-third of the world's population and more than one-quarter of its area. In the overwhelmingly greater part of this added field the Common Law operates under conditions vitally different, in one way or another, from the conditions

---

[1] For a discussion of the exact meaning of this supremacy see pp. 523–4 below.

[2] By repercussion draftsmen tend to concern themselves with minutiae, so that their intention may be manifest in every particular instance to upset the hydra-headed presumptions of the courts in favour of the Common Law. Thus parliament tends to enact the trees, not the wood. A recent instance of the shipwreck of legislation whose general intention was clear is *Rose* v. *Ford*, [1936] 1 K.B.

[3] *West Rand Mining Co.* v. *R.* [1905] 2 K.B. 391; *Rustomjee* v. *R.* 2 Q.B.D. 69; *Mortensen* v. *Peters*, 14 S.L.T. 227. Contrast Art. 6. 2 of the Constitution of the United States.

[4] 'For *jura naturae sunt immutabilia*, and they are *leges legum*.'

of its nurture. It has to mix with alien systems, to cope with unfamiliar institutions, to govern, and even to be administered by, men of strange races, strange loyalties, and strange creeds. How does this very insular product suffer such transplantation? In its new environments does it remain copious, unsociable, and strong? It is the purpose of this chapter to sketch in outline an answer to these questions, in so far as they concern that aspect of the British Empire which is called the British Commonwealth.

The British Commonwealth is only one of two political constellations whose law springs in large measure from the Law of England. The American colonists fought their War of Independence in the name of a not wholly indefensible theory of the Common Law, and Britain took her stand on another.[1] The victory of the colonists resulted in a partition of the Common Law world; but the Americans in their new unit rather exalted than abandoned their Common Law heritage, forging for themselves a federation which fetters policy at every turn by law. Having thus found insistence upon the strictness of the law a two-edged weapon, Great Britain, for the regulation of the Second British Empire, abandoned Declaratory Acts and the strictness of the law in favour of departmental discretion and tacit agreements to let well alone. And when these practices did harden into rules, they became not law but 'convention'.[2]

Meanwhile the law of the imperial relationship, especially that part of it which covered the future Commonwealth, was rusting in comparative disuse. The only great statute of general imperial constitutional law passed in the nineteenth century was the Colonial Laws Validity Act of 1865,[3] and it was occasioned not by any desire of the imperial government to clarify or amend the law, but by the necessity of upsetting the eccentric decisions of a South Australian judge.[4] The courts were a little more active than the legislature, and a couple of dozen leading cases on imperial law might be named. If to these are added the opinions of the law officers of the Crown on colonial subjects,[5] we have all the chief sources of nineteenth-century imperial law. While the Empire strode forward politically, its law stood still. The rules which it needed—for no institution can do without

---

[1] For accounts of the American and English theories, see above, pp. 6–13; McIlwain. *The American Revolution*; Keith, *Constitutional History of the First British Empire*, ch. xiv; and Kennedy, *Essays in Constitutional Law*, ch. i.

[2] In Dicey's sense of the word, which, originally rather inappropriate, is now irrevocably current. See below, p. 60, for a definition of this sense.

[3] 28 & 29 Vict. c. 63.

[4] Boothby, J., who declared large numbers of colonial statutes invalid for repugnancy to English law.

[5] Some of which are published in Forsyth's collection.

rules of some sort—it formulated in another language and with other sanctions, the language and sanctions of constitutional convention. When, therefore, the Empire became the Commonwealth of Nations, its fundamental law was still in all substantial respects the law of George III, the same law which lost Britain the American colonies.

In 1921 the immersion of a foreign body, the Irish Free State, disturbed the quiet waters of the Conventional Commonwealth. Out of the ferment which it created the Statute of Westminster, 1931,[1] emerged. The Statute of Westminster is all that there is of the Commonwealth in law, and it is not very much. Some institutions— the League of Nations, with which the British Commonwealth is often compared, is a striking example—exist in law before they exist in fact.[2] The British Commonwealth took the law by surprise. This was not remarkable, for it had already taken many of its own statesmen by surprise. Had the Commonwealth in 1931 found its lawgiver, as five years earlier it had found its philosopher in Lord Balfour, the leeway might have been made up. But it did not, and the Statute, however creative in the political sphere, brought a purely negative contribution in law.

In this sphere, then, the Common Law has not been 'copious'. The Commonwealth as it now exists is a singularly lawless association. Certainly, the majesty of the Common Law of England is reflected with little diminution of its glory in the judicial institutions of each of the Dominions. But it shines in each separately; their relations with each other are shrouded in a mist of convention. The Commonwealth is even more lawless, though certainly less disorderly, than the comity of nations, for the nations have at least rules of international law which are copious though not observed. The Commonwealth has its habits and usages, which sometimes amount to 'conventional' rules, and it does on the whole observe them; but they are not rules of law.

This nebulous state of the general law of the Empire throws into relief the success of the Common Law within each particular dominion or dependency. Here it has been fruitful, copious, and strong. When, by reason of its unsociable character, it has come into conflict or rivalry with another system of law, it has usually had the better of the difference. In some parts of the Empire the whole of the

[1] 22 Geo. 5, c. 4.
[2] The reference is here to the central function of the League Covenant as a rudimentary international constitution for the prevention of war and the regulation of peace, not to its important subsidiary activities.

standing *corpus* of the law is English law; in others a foreign system exists alongside English law; in others the whole private law belongs to another legal tradition. But even in these last the English public law, the English manner of interpreting statutes, the English law of evidence, and the English system of precedent, intrude in some degree.[1]

But first it is necessary to pursue two aspects of the history of the extension of English law to the colonies: the extension of the English system as a whole, so far as applicable, to settled colonies, and the inevitable extension of a part of British public law to all territories under direct British sovereignty. These two topics will be followed only in the general law of the Empire as declared by British courts, not in their local development in the several colonies, however important; and the general constitutional development of the colonies, a subject which has been often enough expounded, will not be described.

The general law of the modern British Empire springs from and is continuous with the doctrine which the courts of England tardily, under pressure of fact, built up concerning the seventeenth-century 'plantations' in America and 'factories' in the Orient and Africa which Englishmen founded or conquered from other European Powers. To the legal theory of the medieval empire of the Kings of England (Normandy, the Channel Islands, Wales, Ireland, Gascony, Guienne, Calais, Berwick, &c.) the law of the new colonies owed no clear rules except the negative one that the conquest of a country does not necessarily destroy the legal system there existing and substitute that of the conqueror.[2] But the medieval law did offer theories of the absence of any territorial limitation to the Common Law[3] or to the authority of parliament[4] which became fundamental

---

[1] Only where, as in some protectorates and territories under 'indirect rule', native law is administered by native courts under native quasi-sovereignty, is there no element of the Common Law present. But even there the native courts are restrained by the suzerain from infringing 'natural justice', and natural justice as seen by a British Resident will often bear a close resemblance to the fundamental principles of the Common Law.

[2] For this rule see, e.g., Vaughan C.J.'s note on *Process into Wales*, in Vaugh. 395 (which was in fact an undelivered judgment in *Whitrong* v. *Blaney* (1674) 2 Mod. 10); and *Blankard* v. *Galdy* (1694) 2 Salk. 411.

[3] This appears, e.g., from Coke's two propositions that allegiance 'cannot be circumscribed within the predicament of *ubi*' and that '*ligeantia* [allegiance] *est quasi legis essentia*': *Calvin's Case* (1608) 7 Co. Rep. 1a, at 7b, and 4b. *Ergo*, there is nothing in the nature of the Common Law to limit it territorially.

[4] Schuyler, *Parliament and the British Empire*, pp. 36–7. James I sought to exclude parliament from colonial affairs: Keith, *Constitutional History of the First*

in the law of the new colonies. The medieval precedents on these
points were less unambiguous than they were made to appear in the
rationalizations of seventeenth-century Whig lawyers; but the Whig
rationalizations prevailed, and were firmly established by the Revolution of 1689. To the legal theory of the personal union between
England and Scotland, whose *locus classicus* is *Calvin's Case*,[1] the
law of the colonies owed nothing. Observing the close similarity
between the modern conventional-legal theory of the Commonwealth[2]
and Coke's theory of the Union of the Crowns, one is tempted to
speculate what the history of the Empire might have been if the
courts had chosen Scotland instead of Ireland as the precedent for
colonial status. But there was never any likelihood of such a choice,
for the colonies were founded expressly in order to be the economic
dominion of England.[3] One other ostensible source is suggested by
the frequent references in the reports to *ius gentium* and the law of
nature; but these are the merest apology.[4] No rule of international
law really affected decisions; and unless eighteenth-century Whig-
gery be reckoned the law of nature, there is little natural law in the
law of the colonies, though there is plenty of common sense.

Campbell v. *Hall*[5] was decided on the principles of the Glorious
Revolution. In settling the fundamental principles of English nationality, feudal principles were followed.[6] Apart from these matters
there is remarkably little that is doctrinaire in early colonial law.
The law grew up around the plantations and factories; they were not
planned and founded within an existing law. Always the law followed
the facts at a respectful distance.

The two leading rules of the law of colonization furnish good
examples of this empirical process. The first is the rule that a con-

British Empire, pp. 5 sqq. And the Barbados asserted their independence of Crom-
well's authority: Schuyler, op. cit., pp. 110 sqq. But after the Restoration Parliament was left in full exercise of the power until the American Revolution.

[1] (1608) 7 Co. Rep. 1*a*.

[2] See, e.g., Schlosberg, *The King's Republics* (1927), which carried the view of the
Commonwealth as a personal union farther than the law at the time warranted.
See below, p. 526.

[3] For the relations of Scotland to the colonies during the Union of the Crowns,
see below, p. 517.

[4] The Roman law of the acquisition of *res nullius* by occupation was occasionally
cited to justify the exercise of sovereignty over plantations; and the law of nations
was often invoked for the 'principle' that the lives of the conquered were in the hands
of the conquerors.

[5] (1774) Lofft 655, 1 Cowp. 204, 20 St. Tr. 239. This *cause célèbre* decided that once
the Crown has definitely granted representative institutions to a conquered colony
its power to legislate for that colony by Order In Council ceases.

[6] *Calvin's Case* (1608) 7 Co. Rep. 1*a*; *Craw* v. *Ramsey* (1669) Vaugh. 274. See
below, p. 520.

quered or ceded colony retains its previous law (with certain exceptions to be mentioned later)[1] except in so far as the Crown may alter it.[2] This rule is variously justified in the decisions, and has, as we have seen, some medieval authority,[3] but at all times its real ground has been the fact that conquered and ceded territories have been actually left in possession of their 'ancient laws'.

The other leading rule is that, when Englishmen found a colony in an uninhabited or savage[4] country, they carry with them the English law so far as it is applicable. This rule appears to have rested, not on the express provisions for the introduction of English law which were often, though not always, inserted in the charters,[5] nor upon the circumstance that the charters usually included a grant of the colonial land to be held of the English Crown 'as of our Manor of East Greenwich',[6] but on a vague attachment of English law to the persons of Englishmen, at least so long as they did not subject themselves to the law of another sovereign.[7] The process, therefore, by

[1] See below, pp. 518–20. Coke's exception, that the laws of infidels cease altogether, was qualified in *Blankard* v. *Galdy* (1694) 2 Salk. 411, 412, Comb. 225, and in the case of 1722 before the Privy Council referred to in 2 P. Will. 75. It was repudiated with undeserved vehemence by Lord Mansfield in *Campbell* v. *Hall* (1774) Lofft 655, 741. The case which it was intended to cover, that is to say, the acquisition of territories whose existing system of law is such that Englishmen cannot reasonably be expected to conform to it, is now in effect covered by the special rules as to Oriental 'factories', for which see below, p. 518.

[2] The leading dictum is that of Coke in *Calvin's Case* (1608) 7 Co. Rep. 1a, 17b. The Crown may alter the 'ancient law' by the terms of the capitulation: *Campbell* v. *Hall*, Lofft 655, 741; and the commander of the conquering forces has full power to arrange any terms of capitulation he pleases. After capitulation the Crown may legislate by order-in-council: *Forbes* v. *Cochrane* (1824) 2 B. & C. 448, by letters patent or charter: *Campbell* v. *Hall*, above; *Jephson* v. *Riera* (1835) 3 Knapp 130, 151, and possibly by order under the sign-manual or by a mere expression of the will of the Secretary of State: *Cameron* v. *Kyte* (1835) 3 Knapp 332; but the Governor alone cannot legislate: ibid.

[3] Above, p. 514.

[4] In theory, the distinction between settlement in savage territory and conquest from infidels (see above, n. 1) might not seem clear, but in practice, territory inhabited by American Indians was reckoned uninhabited, while settlements in Oriental countries were treated as 'factories'. See below, p. 518.

[5] Cf. Chalmers, *Political Annals of the United Colonies* (1780), p. 14, and Keith, *Constitutional History of the First British Empire*, p. 3.

[6] Some colonies were granted to their proprietors with the exceptional status of Counties Palatine.

[7] 'Then taking it as the Truth is, certain subjects of England, by Consent of their Prince, go and possess an uninhabited desert Country; the Common Law must be supposed their rule, as 'twas their Birthright, and as 'tis the best, and so to be presumed their Choice; and not only that, but even as Obligatory, 'tis so. When they went thither, they no more abandoned the English Laws, than they did their natural Allegiance; nay, they subjected themselves thereby no more to other Laws, than they did to another Allegiance, which they did not.' Argument of counsel before the House of Lords in *Dutton* v. *Howell* (1694) Show. Parl. Cas. 24, 32.

which the English law was extended to English settlements was primarily personal, not territorial, and it is always so treated in the authorities.[1] But as soon as the original settlers had reached the colony, their invisible and inescapable cargo of English law fell from their shoulders and attached itself to the soil on which they stood. Their personal law became the territorial law of the colony. Subsequent settlers did not, like the founders, bring with them the law of England as they left it, but entered into the colony as they would into any other country, becoming subject to the established territorial law.[2] Nor, as we have seen, did English law automatically follow Englishmen to colonies conquered from a civilized power.

It is remarkable that after the legislative union with Scotland in 1707, when England and Scotland merged into a single kingdom of Great Britain having two territorially limited systems of private law, equal in status, the law that followed citizens of the united realm to colonies subsequently founded was invariably the law of England.[3] There is nothing in the Acts of Union or elsewhere expressly prescribing this.[4] In fact, Scotland had just failed to establish a Scottish colony in Darien,[5] and her consent to the union with England amounted to a final adoption of the English colonies instead of an empire of her own as the domain of her future trade.[6] Scotsmen accordingly did not question the reflection of this policy in law, and were content to be Englishmen overseas.[7]

---

[1] In the exhaustive argument in *Dutton* v. *Howell*, already cited, counsel urged, *inter alia*, as a ground for the extension of English law to the colonies the rule (*semble*, of international law) that by occupying colonial land settlers acquired it for the Crown, and the fact that colonial land was held of the Crown. This is the only exception.

[2] Statutes subsequent to the settlement did, of course, apply to the colony if they could be construed as *intended* to apply. But prior statutes applied if their nature was such that they were *capable* of applying.

[3] Sir Maurice Amos observes that in capitulatory courts in Egypt, English law is treated as the national law of all British subjects.

[4] Unless, in view of the mercantilist view of colonies then prevailing, the provision in the Acts of Union that the laws of the United Kingdom as to trade should be those of England be thought to cover the point.

[5] Had it succeeded this colony would have been under Scottish sovereignty, as would Nova Scotia, for which a charter was given to Sir William Alexander by James I and VI under the Great Seal of Scotland. This colony also was abortive; Nova Scotia was subsequently acquired under English auspices.

[6] From 1603 to 1707 Scotsmen had the rights of Englishmen as well in the colonies as in England itself. Opinion of Sir John Hawles, S.-G., quoted in Chalmers, *Political Annals of the United Colonies*, p. 259. But Scottish ports did not enjoy the benefit of the Navigation Acts.

[7] Professor R. W. Lee points out as an interesting parallel that in the Dutch East Indian Colonies (including South Africa) the law of the Province of Holland prevailed over the law of any other of the seven provinces of the Netherlands. Cf. Lee, *Introduction to Roman-Dutch Law* (3rd ed.), p. 9, n. 4.

Three exceptions to the rule concerning conquered and ceded colonies are not very clear. One is the special position of Oriental factories.[1] Another is the rule, which seems to be established by *Lindsay* v. *Oriental Bank*,[2] that where it is not definitely shown that an alien system of law applies, the application of the Common Law will be presumed by the Privy Council.[3] Further, *Ruding* v. *Smith*[4] establishes some sort of exception to the dictum in *Campbell* v. *Hall*[5] that 'the law and legislation of every dominion equally effects all persons and property within the limits'.[6]

It remains to discuss the extent to which, during the formative period of the general colonial law, English sovereignty was held to introduce of necessity English public law to colonies which retained other legal systems. By reason of the absence from the British constitution of formally 'entrenched' principles of government, only a small proportion—one might almost say the bare minimum—of English law is so imposed.[7] This minimum has been eloquently defined by Lord Stowell:[8]

> 'No small portion of the ancient law is unavoidably superseded, by the revolution of government that has taken place. The allegiance of the subjects, and all the law that relates to it—the administration of the law in the Sovereign, and appellate jurisdictions—and all the laws connected with the exercise of the sovereign authority—must undergo alterations adapted to the change.'

In the Middle Ages the ambit of jurisdiction was the ambit of law, and the King's law ruled where the King's writs ran. The privileges and subordinations of his realms inferior to England varied with no clear common measure. But here, as elsewhere, it is unnecessary to go into the medieval law because what was authoritative for subse-

---

[1] *The Indian Chief* (1800) 3 Rob. Adm. 22, 28, 31; *Lautour* v. *Teesdale* (1816) 8 Taunt. 830; *Advocate-General of Bengal* v. *Ranee Surnomoyee Dossee* (1863) 2 Moo. P.C. (N.S.) 59; *Papayanni* v. *Russian Steamship Co.* (1863) 2 Moo. P.C. (N.S.) 161.

[2] (1860) 13 Moo. P.C. 401.

[3] This was a curious case, inadequately reported, where one would have expected the Roman-Dutch law to be presumed. It is doubtful if the presumption of the common law would now be applied rigidly.

[4] (1821) 2 Hagg. Cons. 371.

[5] (1774) Lofft 655, 741.

[6] The felicity of Lord Stowell's style in *Ruding* v. *Smith* is only equalled by the ambiguity of its *ratio decidendi*. Probably the case is best treated, as it was in *Armitage* v. *Armitage* (1866) L. R. 3 Eq. 343, as deciding simply that, where compliance with the full local formalities of marriage is impossible, compliance with the formalities of the *lex domicilii* will suffice. On this view, the case decides nothing pertinent to Imperial law as such.

[7] For a striking instance, see *in re Adam* (1887) 1 Moo. P.C. 460.

[8] In *Ruding* v. *Smith* (1821) 2 Hagg. Cons. 371, 382.

quent ages was not the medieval law itself, but what Coke and his seventeenth-century successors, ingenuously or disingenuously, said it had been. Coke distinguished between the writs of private remedies and writs which served to maintain the royal power.[1] The latter alone ran to the Dominions. They included what are now called the prerogative writs[2] and the cognate writ of error, which was in effect a restricted form of appeal.[3] From the first, writs of error were not used for appeals from the colonies, because the administrative jurisdiction of the Privy Council gave an opportunity for a wider and more satisfactory form of appeal. But they and the prerogative writs continued to be available, in strict law, until well into the nineteenth century.[4]

The 'Government and superintendency of the Crown', in the sense in which Vaughan, C.J., spoke of it,[5] came in fact to be maintained, not by the courts of common law through the awkward process of these writs, but by the King's Council itself. At first no distinction was drawn between its administrative and its judicial functions in the supervision of the colonies,[6] but by the end of the seventeenth century they were fairly well separated, though exercised by the same body of persons. Regular reports of cases before the Privy Council were first published in 1829.[7] Despite the transference of the judicial functions from the whole Council to the Judicial Committee constituted by the Acts of 1833 and 1844,[8] this remarkable court retains to the present-day forms of procedure which are appropriate to an administrative rather than to a judicial body. The general case law of the British Empire is almost entirely the creation of the Privy Council.

[1] *Calvin's Case* (1608) 7 Co. Rep. 1a, 9b. Vaughan, C.J., quoting Coke, expounds him thus: 'More intelligibly it may be said, That Writs in order to the Particular Rights and Properties of the Subject (which he called *Brevia mandatoria remedialia*) . . . issue not to the Dominions that are no part of England, but belonging to it: For surely, as they have their particular Laws, so consequently they must have their particular Mandates or Writs in order to them. . . . *Brevia mandatoria, et non remedialia*, are Writs that concern not the particular Rights or Properties of the subject, but the Government and Superintendency of the King, *ne quid res publica capiat detrimenti*': *Process into Wales* (1674) Vaugh., 395, 400.

[2] Habeas corpus, mandamus, prohibition, and certiorari; together with some other miscellaneous writs now mostly obsolete.

[3] See the dictum of Vaughan, C.J., in *Process into Wales* (1674) Vaugh. 395, 402, quoted below, p. 556.

[4] After the decision of the Queen's Bench in *in re Anderson* (1861) 30 L.R. (Q.B.) 129 that the Queen's Bench had jurisdiction to grant habeas corpus to a colonial court, the jurisdiction to grant this writ was abolished by 25 & 26 Vict. c. 20. See further Safford and Wheeler, *Privy Council Practice*, p. 713, n. (k).

[5] Above, n. 1.

[6] See, e.g., *Clayborne's Case* (1638), reported in Chalmers, *Political Annals of the United Colonies*, p. 233.

[7] Knapp's Reports.   [8] 3 & 4 Will. 4, c. 41; 7 & 8 Vict. c. 69.

For the theoretical reason of its close association with the person of the sovereign, and for the same practical reasons which Vaughan, C.J., cites[1] as a ground for the extension of the prerogative writs to the colonies, the jurisdiction of the Privy Council was held to extend to every territory of which the King was sovereign. The present position of this jurisdiction is discussed below.[2]

The sovereignty of the King, wherever it went, was held to carry with it a uniform law of allegiance. Although the actual importance of the law of nationality lies in the differentiation of the status of nationals and non-nationals for numerous purposes of public and private law, allegiance is in sentiment and in theory a direct and reciprocal relationship of king and subject, and is often spoken of as constituting the moral or philosophical basis of all municipal law.[3] At least, that was the view of seventeenth-century theory, which treated the King's protection as the correlative of the subject's obedience.[4] Accordingly, it was the law of the Crown of England— the common law or Imperial statute—which determined in all parts of the Empire alike whether a man was or was not a British subject.[5] But the rights and liabilities attached to that status were, and are, a matter of local law.[6] There is nothing to prevent the local law from conferring upon an alien or a class of aliens rights identical, within the territory, with those of British subjects. Naturalization in a subordinate dominion amounts, in effect, to this.[7]

The jurisdiction of the Privy Council and the law of allegiance do not only differ from the general common law in that they are introduced equally into all colonies by the mere fact of British sovereignty, but also in that they are immune from alteration by local legislative organs unless these are specifically empowered to that end by the Imperial parliament. They therefore constitute, from the colonial point of view, a sort of Imperial fundamental law, which will, amongst other things, be discussed in the next section.[8]

[1] Below, p. 556.
[2] Section II (2).
[3] 'Ligeantia . . . est quasi essentia legis': *Calvin's Case* (1608) 7 Co. Rep. 1*a*, 4*b*.
[4] Ibid., at 5*a*; *Dutton* v. *Howell* (1694) Show. Parl. Cas. 24, 32.
[5] *Donegani* v. *Donegani* (1835) 3 Knapp 63; *in re Adam* (1857) 1 Moo. P.C. 460.
[6] *Donegani* v. *Donegani*; *in re Adam*.
[7] Local naturalization is no new thing. The rule was established in *Craw* v. *Ramsey* (1669) Vaugh. 274, a case which concerned naturalization in Ireland before the Union. Though the grounds of the decision might not now be accepted, the result is good law. That is to say, the general powers of self-government which a modern Dominion has do not include the power to grant a British nationality which will be valid all over the Empire. This can be done only under the British Nationality and Status of Aliens Act 1914. Cf. *Markwald* v. *Attorney-General*, [1920] 1 Ch. 348.
[8] Section II (3).

II

UNITY IN COMMONWEALTH LAW

The heading of this section is no more than a vague rubric to cover some inquiries, selected arbitrarily for their interest rather than for exhaustiveness, into certain general phenomena in Commonwealth law. It will appear—as has already been foreshadowed in the foregoing section—that of recent years the law of the Commonwealth has been a by-product or epiphenomenon of its politics. For this reason, although the relation of various kinds of legal unity to the political cohesion of the Commonwealth will be discussed, they will not be approached primarily as 'bonds of Empire'. It is not assumed that it is either desirable or undesirable that the Empire should have bonds, or even that, given the desirability of bonds in general, legal bonds should or should not figure among them. It will rather appear from the ensuing discussion that the law is now incapable of supplying significant bonds, that in the present state of the Commonwealth the degree of its unity in law has no organic relation to its political unity. A succeeding section will consider the other régimes, the other principles of order in Commonwealth affairs, which present themselves as alternatives to strict law. All that will here be shown is that legal unity of any sort is not now a goal to be striven for by imperialists as such. The topics discussed in this section are so grouped merely by reason of their common historical derivation from the system which has been described in the last section.

Apology is perhaps due for the extent to which these discussions trespass upon philosophy on the one hand and politics on the other. But the general law of the Commonwealth is not ordinary law. It lies rather on the periphery of municipal law, where it marches with politics, with 'constitutional convention', and with international law. Questions on the margin of a subject necessarily stir more extraneous issues than do points which lie comfortably in the centre of established doctrine; in such frontier regions to require self-sufficiency of legal scholarship is to ensure not its chastity but its sterility.

One more prefatory warning or exculpation must be made. A simple pragmatic view of the nature of law is assumed throughout: that that only is law which is declared and enforced by the courts, or will be declared and applied by the courts if occasion arises; where it is not applied, it is not law. This is not the place to justify that definition; indeed, it is not for all purposes a satisfactory definition of law. But it has for the present purpose at least this merit, that it is the implicit traditional theory of English law, though possibly not of British speculation.

1. *Formal Unity.*

Every community has a multiplicity of authorities issuing rules and orders, general and particular, which have the force of law. For both practical and theoretical reasons it is of primary importance that these rules and orders should not contradict each other: that is to say, that the citizen should not be placed in the position of having to obey requirements of the law which are inconsistent with each other. Only to the extent that provision is made for resolving apparent conflicts of this nature does an agglomeration of laws become a *system* of law.[1]

The resolution of such conflicts is effected, and consistently with the nature of law can only be effected, by inquiring of each purported rule of law: by what authority does it speak? From what source is its legal character, its quality of being law, derived? The answer will always take the form of a more general proposition of law which, from the point of view of validity, is logically prior to the rule examined, and from which the validity of the rule can accordingly be deduced. Behind the prior rule a still more general rule will be discoverable, and so on. The relative validity of conflicting rules will be determined when a prior rule is reached from which both derive their validity. Analysis need then go no farther. But theory allows and practice may require the pursuit of the analysis to a point at which a proposition is found which is ultimate in law—behind which stands no prior legal proposition, but whose validity depends on non-legal considerations.[2] Such a rule is called by Kelsen a *Grundnorm.*[3]

---

[1] *Rechtsordnung* (Kelsen). The whole of the preliminary analysis upon which this discussion of formal unity rests is derived from Kelsen. But the adoption of Kelsen's calculus of formal validity and of his Kantian *a priori* derivation of it must not be taken to commit the writer to Kelsen's estimate of the actual importance of the purely rational or formal element in law. See Kelsen: *Allgemeine Staatslehre* (1925), pp. 248–51.

[2] The nature of the non-legal considerations which are called upon to justify obedience to law as such by the theorist, by the conscientious citizen seeking a reason for his obedience to the State, or by the judge examining the postulates of his office vary infinitely, and include considerations of ethics, religion, political principle, tradition, and mere blind reflex loyalty. They are preponderantly inexplicit in legal systems of long standing like that of Great Britain, and explicit by comparison where conflicts between systems have rendered the acceptance of judicial office, and even of the duties of citizenship, something like a choice between real alternatives.

[3] 'Ground-norm', or 'foundation-norm'. A norm in Kelsen's sense is a proposition of the form '*A* is, therefore *B* ought to be', where *A* and *B* are situations of fact (*Tatbestände*).

The *Grundnorm* is the ground of the validity of the system which depends on it, and its supremacy constitutes the assurance that there will be no conflict within that system. It may therefore be said to embody and express the formal unity of the system. From the point of view of their form, of their validity, all other rules in the system are particularizations of the *Grundnorm*.

It is usual in English constitutional writings, whose tacit.jurisprudence is Austin's theory of law as command, to find the ultimate formal source of law in a dynamic authority, the 'sovereign', rather than in a static principle, the *Grundnorm*. A *Grundnorm* in the simple form *quod principi placuit legis habet vigorem*, that is to say, a *Grundnorm* prescribir~ simply that the sovereign is the sole source of authority, and .entifying him, is *prima facie* conceivable, and may even have existed in some system of law. It would seem accordingly that Austinian sovereignty might be a legitimate special case under Kelsen's general theory of the *Grundnorm*.[1] But modern criticism makes it doubtful whether even the British constitution is exactly that special case. Where the purported sovereign is any one but a single actual person,[2] the designation of him must include the statement of rules for the ascertainment of his will,[3] and these rules, since their observance is a condition of the validity of his legislation, are rules of law logically prior to him.[4] Further, the mere assertion of the omnipotence of a sovereign leaves completely uncertain the fundamental question whether or not he can bind himself; but the addition of a ruling in either sense on this point makes the basic rule of the system something more than a mere designation of the sovereign. Thus even the theoretic possibility of sovereignty as a *Grundnorm* is questionable. But however that may be, and however happy the Austinian theory may be in its application to the British constitution, it manifestly breaks down when applied to a constitu-

---

[1] Professor C. A. W. Manning in his essay on Austin almost asserts this: *Modern Theories of Law* (Oxford University Press, 1933), pp. 192 sqq.

The word is cumbrous, but has no exact short equivalent in English; the nearest is 'basic rule'. Hereinafter the word *Grundnorm* will only be used where it is necessary to insist on the fact, expounded above, that the fundamental thing in a system of law is a *proposition*. Elsewhere it will be more seemly to speak of the 'root' of a system of law—an expression for which the writer is indebted to Meredith, J., in *Cahill* v. *Attorney-General*, quoted below, p. 536.

[2] Whether a body unincorporate, a corporation aggregate, or even a corporation sole. Where the succession to even the rankest despot is disputed, questions of fundamental law arise.

[3] Thus, the King, Lords, and Commons meeting in a single joint assembly, and voting by majority, or even unanimously, could not enact a statute.

[4] On this and the next point see *Attorney-General of New South Wales* v. *Trethowan*, [1932] A.C. 526; and Jennings, *The Law and the Constitution*, ch. iv.

tion where either a partition of powers between different authorities or fundamental guarantees are 'entrenched' behind a procedure of amendment more difficult than the process of ordinary legislation.[1] Here the *Grundnorm*, whether or not it coincides with the written constitution, is clearly prior and superior to the legislature and is daily so treated by the courts. The theory of the *Grundnorm*, then, provides a general scheme or calculus of the formal validity of law, a scheme, moreover, which follows inevitably from the nature of law itself. The theory of the sovereign, at best, provides neither. It is, however, approximately true for countries with unitary constitutions, and in general the language of the approximate theory is readily translatable into the language of the true theory. So in the next page or two the reader who boggles at exotic analysis will not err greatly if he understands identity and difference of *Grundnorm* as referring to identity and difference of sovereign.

That a system of law should have a *Grundnorm* is, as we have seen, implicit in the nature of law. But in practice this means merely that the existence of *some* single common *Grundnorm* is assumed whenever a body of law is treated as a coherent system, not that in order that any law shall be valid it must be shown that a *Grundnorm* has been explicitly formulated and that the law is derived from it. Where the constitution is written and law is codified, the *Grundnorm* may be explicit from the beginning. But in the English system of case-law fundamental principles are not stated, and the judicial process is not purely deductive. The data of the law are *rationes decidendi* of previously decided cases, which stand midway between the generality of the broader provisions of a code and the utter particularity of decisions 'on the facts'. Principles more general than existing *rationes decidendi* are ascertained, ostensibly by the process which logicians call induction, as and when they are required to explain existing decisions and to deal with situations not covered by existing authority. Once so ascertained, a principle becomes the *ratio decidendi* of the case in which it is ascertained and is established as an authority for future cases. Clearly in such a system there is no certainty that the most fundamental principle, the *Grundnorm*, will be reached and declared by the courts. It may be that no case will arise which necessitates resort to the ultimate rule. Yet at any time such a case may arise, for by definition the *Grundnorm* is a rule of law, and, also by

[1] Where there is only a partition of powers, the *Grundnorm* is complex, but still purely formal. Where there are constitutional guarantees, the *Grundnorm* is substantial as well as formal: it determines not only the validity but also some of the content of the rules of law below.

definition, since it is a rule of law, it must be capable of declaration and application by the courts.

In fact, such judicial induction is by no means pure ;[1] indeed, it is naturally even more impure than judicial deduction is now universally conceded to be.[2] In both processes the general outlook of the judge is a powerful tacit major premise. This is particularly true in a field as little tilled by judicial decision as the ultimate constitutional theory of the Common Law. That this field is unexplored in England may be seen from the striking fact that Dicey was unable to cite a single decided case as authority for his classic exposition of the sovereignty of Parliament.[3] The courts entrusted with judicial review of legislation in the federal Dominions have to venture farther into the abstract and general, but still contrive to pitch their *rationes decidendi* fairly low.[4] Even so, the influence of their judges' general philosophies stands out more strongly in high constitutional decisions than in decisions on ordinary private law.[5] If this tendency is so marked at the penultimate degree, it is to be expected that decisions on the ultimate question, decisions defining the *Grundnorm*, will reflect still more strongly the basic beliefs of the judges themselves. It may then be said, and not in any cynical way, that the *Grundnorm* of a case-law system is simply the sum of those principles which command the ultimate allegiance of the courts. This loose definition opens up possibilities of indeterminacy of *Grundnorm* and of shifting of *Grundnorm* which will be illustrated in the next few pages.

Our purpose is to ascertain the extent to which there is formal unity in Commonwealth law. To this end it is fortunately not necessary to attempt to state the British or any other *Grundnorm*,[6] but only to discover whether all or any of the members of the Commonwealth share a common *Grundnorm*, whatever its terms may be. The

[1] If, indeed, any induction is pure, which logicians doubt.

[2] If their logic were pure, judges could not exercise their salutary function of creating case law.

[3] Dicey, *Law of the Constitution*, ch. i.

[4] *Trethowan's Case*, already cited, is an instance where the diffidence of the Privy Council amounted to timidity. The Board avoided a fundamental issue, squarely raised, by a decision 'on the words of the Statute'.

[5] The judgments of Isaacs and Higgins, JJ., on the Australian Constitution are a notable instance. Isaacs, J., was in the habit of stating with unusual fullness the considerations which influenced him.

[6] The limits within which the British *Grundnorm* must lie are, however, clear. It must assign supremacy in some sense to Parliament, and recognize, subject to that supremacy, the Common Laws of England and Scotland and the Prerogative. The only point outstanding is the extent to which Parliament may bind itself, as to which see above, p. 523, and Jennings, loc. cit.

fact that the *Grundnormen* we seek may be—and, as we shall discover, are—inexplicit hinders our task, but does not frustrate it. But
first it is convenient to eliminate two possible sources of misunder-
standing. In the first place, though the fact that the appellate
jurisdiction of the Privy Council extends to a Dominion assists the
maintenance of formal unity, it is not conclusive in its favour.[1] In
the second place, the fact that the Imperial Parliament retains recognized legislative functions in relation to a Dominion, such as the
amendment of the British North America Act,[2] may be consistent
with a difference of *Grundnorm*. For already, in constitutional convention, the Imperial Parliament exercises these powers not on its
own behalf, but as the mere agent of the Dominion. It is not at all
impossible that the law of a Dominion should come to regard the
Imperial Parliament's legislative power within the borders of the
Dominion as now derivative—delegated by tolerance, if not expressly[3]—if only it can explain how its former supremacy was termi-
nated.

Formal unity of law clearly exists between England, Scotland,
and Northern Ireland, despite the partial bifurcation in legislative
authority between Great Britain and Northern Ireland and the partial
severance of Scots private law from that of the rest of the United
Kingdom. The law of the dependent Empire of the United Kingdom,
with the curious exception of the Indian States and certain other
subordinate monarchies, clearly shares the same root. Newfoundland
and New Zealand, Dominions which have never been strongly nationalist, have always looked to the United Kingdom for the formal source of
their law.[4] Australia does likewise, not from lack of nationalism, but
because Australian nationalism has always been interested rather in
the substance than in the trappings and formal guarantees of independence.[5] If, however, Australia should at any time want to sever
her law from the Imperial root, the nature of her federal system
would create serious difficulties. Since the constitutions of the Com-

---

[1] For the relation of jurisdictional unity to formal unity, see below, pp. 543–5.

[2] And, *a fortiori*, the power of the Imperial Parliament to legislate for a Dominion
with its request and consent, under s. 4 of the Statute of Westminster.

[3] This view was taken, prematurely perhaps, by Mr. Schlosberg in 1927: H. J.
Schlosberg, *The King's Republics* (Stevens, 1927), pp. 21, 57, 68.

[4] Newfoundland was in 1933, at the request of her Government and Parliament,
deprived of her self-governing constitution and put under a Commission, by Act of
the Imperial Parliament: 24 & 25 Geo. V, c. 2. This is her present status.

[5] The reluctance with which an eminent Australian lawyer finds himself forced to
realize that the Imperial *Grundnorm* is anywhere questioned as the root of Dominion
law may be seen in Mr. Justice Dixon's address in 10 *Aust. Law Journ., Supp.* 96.
See also the Commonwealth Attorney-General, ibid., p. 108.

monwealth and the States are not contained in a single instrument, but in so many separate Acts of the Imperial Parliament, there is no measure within Australia of the mutual status of the parties to Federation. Accordingly, if the Imperial Parliament ceased to be looked to as the original source of law, there would have to be a novation of the federal compact, a new fundamental agreement between Commonwealth and States.[1] But the situation is most unlikely to occur.

Despite the more meticulous temper of Canadian nationalism, it does not seek to deny history by repudiating the Imperial root of Canadian law.[2] Dissatisfaction with the legal status of Canada takes less high ground, and attacks the Privy Council appeal and the role of the Imperial Parliament in amending the Canadian constitution. As has been suggested above, these bonds, even while they continue, are not an insuperable obstacle to a breach of formal unity, but they are a serious discouragement. But if Canada does ever desire to establish a local root for her law, her federal system will offer no obstacles comparable to those in Australia, since the British North America Act is the constitution alike of the Dominion and of the Provinces.[3]

It is impossible to understand the constitutional policy of South Africa without reference to political conditions. South African nationalism is strong, developed, and legalistic, but not fanatical.[4] The peculiar objective of moderate South African nationalists has been the 'right of secession'. Like all legal or pseudo-legal terms which become the ammunition of political controversy, this phrase has been misused. It is in any case permissible to doubt whether the formula was ever a happy one to express the real desire of those

---

[1] The difficulties experienced in adapting the emancipatory provisions of the Statute of Westminster to Australia spring from the same source. The adaptation has been very imperfectly done, and will cause difficulties when the Statute is adopted by Australia. See W. A. Wynes, *Legislative and Executive Powers in Australia* (Law Book Co. of Australia, 1936), pp. 73–87.

[2] But for a suggestion by a Canadian scholar that in deciding *British Coal Corporation* v. *R.*, [1935] A.C. 500, the Judicial Committee of the Privy Council should have treated the Report of the Imperial Conference of 1926 as a first source of Canadian sovereign status in law, see Dean V. C. Macdonald in 13 Can. Bar Rev. 625. Compare this view with the South African developments discussed below.

[3] Dr. Maurice Ollivier, however, has suggested that Canada should assert her formal independence by enacting an amended Constitution in advance of imperial legislation approving thereof: *L'Avenir Constitutionnel du Canada* (Montreal, 1935), p. 150.

[4] 'The Afrikaner's forbears were Dutchmen, a people great in law and polemical theology, French Huguenots, of all men most logical, and West Germans, a highly schematic folk' (*Round Table*, vol. xviii, p. 651).

who used it. What the majority of them desired was rather freedom to secede if they should so wish—a purely political objective.

More precisely, the substance of their demand was for assurance that if the white South African nation should unequivocally declare its intention to secede from the Commonwealth, no compulsive or punitive action would in fact be taken by any other member of the Commonwealth, in the name of the law or otherwise, to frustrate the translation of that intention into fact. Without such freedom in fact, a legal right of secession would be useless. This freedom once assured, there was little that the establishment of the legal right could add. Yet there were two ways in which the legal right might buttress the political freedom. In the first place, it is conceivable, though not likely, that, if all other influences left the issue in the balance, Great Britain's decision whether to intervene actively might be determined by the British Government's view of the legality of secession.[1] In the second place—and this is a matter of importance among a people as law-abiding as most South African citizens are—it would hinder a movement for actual secession at all its stages, and might lead to some citizens withholding their loyalty from the Union after it was accomplished, if it could be said that secession was in the strict law of South Africa illegal.[2] If, on the other hand, secession were legal, the stigma of revolution would attach not to the secessionists but to those who refused to accept secession. Those nationalists who consciously intended in claiming the right of secession to claim something more than freedom to secede must be supposed to have had these considerations in mind.

Until their fusion in 1934 there was a line of cleavage between the two principal parties on 'the Imperial issue'. The Nationalist Party held, before 1926, that the right of secession did not exist, and ought to be established. After 1926, General Hertzog, its leader, held that the right of secession had been acquired at the Imperial Conference, while other members of the party thought that it was not yet secure. The South African Party, led by General Smuts, considered it not worth seeking, thinking that South Africa would best secure her substantial freedom by adhering firmly to the British Commonwealth. General Smuts differed from General Hertzog over the effect of the resolutions of the 1926 Imperial Conference, holding

---

[1] The point is of course unreal. At no time since the Great War has there been any possibility that Great Britain would actively oppose South African secession. But we are here seeking to find a meaning for the views of those who thought that there was such a possibility.

[2] It is probably no less true that the knowledge that secession is legal is likely to rob of its zest any movement for secession. But this does not affect the argument.

that they did not confer a right of secession in law. With the situation, so understood, his party was content. The enactment of the Statute of Westminster in 1931 made no difference in these alignments beyond increasing the confidence of the Nationalist Party in its view.

In 1933, however, the Nationalist and South African Parties made a coalition, which was followed in 1934 by fusion. The basis of the coalition, so far as constitutional policy was concerned, was an agreement that membership of the British Commonwealth should be accepted without reserve (which meant that actual secession would no longer be contemplated), but that South Africa should be shown unequivocally to have, within the Commonwealth, full freedom, formal as well as substantial (which implied, though they may not have admitted it in public, abandonment by South African party coalitionists of their opposition to the establishment of the formal right of secession). The Union Government was thus in effect commissioned to remove all vestiges of formal subordination of South Africa to the United Kingdom, subject to two overriding considerations: that the institutions to which Commonwealth sentiment properly attached (that is, in effect, the Crown) should not be attacked, and that good relations with the United Kingdom should not be even slightly disturbed.

The existing situation was not satisfactory by these standards. Apart altogether from minor provisions of the South Africa Act implying subordination, and the major question of the 'entrenched clauses',[1] the central issue of the right of secession was still outstanding. The Statute of Westminster, standing alone, was open to a construction which would make secession legal,[2] but it could not

[1] All these points have been 'cleaned up' by amendments of the South Africa Act by the Union Parliament. The 'entrenched clauses' have been removed from the fundamental law of the Union and converted into a solemn international obligation of good faith.

[2] There is, it is submitted with respect, no substance in Professor Keith's contention (*The King and the Imperial Crown* (Longmans, 1936), p. 449) that the preamble to the Statute of Westminster has the effect of rendering secession conventionally impossible. No preamble is an enactment of law. This exceptional preamble is a declaration of convention. There are no established canons of interpretation of declarations of constitutional convention. But since such a declaration derives any force it has from the *consensus* of the parties, it must be legitimate to look, in construing it, at the intention of the parties. It is notorious that two at least of the Dominions who in 1930 consented to the draft of this preamble did not regard it as establishing a convention prohibiting secession, and would not have consented to it in that sense. The South Africans actually declared that the right of secession was not to be taken to be prejudiced, and the declaration was noted by the Imperial Conference. In any case, would a law terminating the allegiance of a Dominion to the Throne be a law 'touching the Succession to the Throne'? In the first place, the Throne, in convention as in law, is a single throne. Its existence as a throne and the

be contended that it unequivocally did so. Yet a request for a further emancipatory Imperial statute so soon after the Statute of Westminster would not have been well received in the United Kingdom. But in any case there was this further difficulty, that established constitutional doctrine held that it was in strict law impossible for the Imperial Parliament to put it beyond its own power to repeal any of its own Acts.[1] Any measure of emancipation at the hands of the Imperial Parliament would therefore suffer from the vital flaw that it was revocable at the Imperial Parliament's pleasure. According to established theory, nothing that Westminster could do would remove this taint from its gifts. In other words, the revocability in strict law of Dominion emancipation seemed to be ineradicable so long as South African law adhered to its Imperial root. Accordingly, South African law had to be detached from its Imperial root without offending Great Britain. Escape from this dilemma demanded both courage and tact. Neither were wanting, and a delicate and radical stratagem was found, of whose success it is still too early to judge.

There has been in South Africa since 1926 a legal heresy which may be called the nationalist theory of status. This theory in the first place took a very wide view of the Balfour Report, regarding it as establishing or recognizing the complete independence of the Dominions within the Commonwealth—as was legitimate and, in the event, correct. The heresy consisted in treating the terms of the Report, thus construed, as themselves valid in constitutional law. It was clearly authoritative in constitutional convention, and it is arguable that it affected international law.[2] But convention, by definition, leaves the law intact; and British law, which on this point is also the law of the Dominions,[3] does not allow international law to intrude into municipal law unless expressly adopted.[4] Responsible scholars, including those of nationalist views in politics, did not adopt this obviously untenable view.[5] If such a fundamental change in the law of South Africa had occurred, it would hardly have passed unnoticed by either the legislature or the courts. A cognate but lesser

rules of succession to it are unaffected by the number of realms that owe it allegiance. In the second place, would even the abolition of all allegiance to the Throne be a change in the law relating to the succession to it?

[1] Dicey, *Law of the Constitution*, ch. i; for criticism see Jennings, *The Law and the Constitution*, ch. iv, and above, p. 525.

[2] On the effect of the Balfour Report upon the status of the Dominions in international law see P. J. Noel Baker, *The Juridical Status of the British Dominions in International Law*, ch. v, pp. 130 sqq.

[3] Except possibly the Irish Free State.

[4] *West Rand Central Gold Mining Co.* v. *R.*, [1905] 2 K.B. 391.

[5] e.g. Schlosberg, *The King's Republics*, ch. ix.

heresy is that the Statute of Westminster translated the constitutional declarations of 1926 *en masse* into law.

In 1934 the Union Parliament enacted the Status of the Union Act 1934,[1] the preamble whereof runs as follows in the English text:

WHEREAS the delegates of His Majesty's Governments in the United Kingdom, the Dominion of Canada, the Commonwealth of Australia, the Dominion of New Zealand, the Union of South Africa, the Irish Free State and Newfoundland, at Imperial Conferences holden at Westminster in the years of our Lord 1926 and 1930, did concur in making the declarations and resolutions set forth in the Reports of the said Conferences, and more particularly in defining the group of self-governing communities composed of Great Britain and the Dominions as 'autonomous communities within the British Empire, equal in status, in no way subordinate one to another in any aspect of their domestic or external affairs, though united by a common allegiance to the Crown and freely associated as members of the British Commonwealth of Nations';

And whereas the said resolutions and declarations in so far as they required legislative sanction on the part of the United Kingdom have been ratified, confirmed and established by the Parliament of the United Kingdom in an Act entitled the Statute of Westminster, 1931 (22 Geo. V, c. 4);

And whereas it is expedient that the status of South Africa as a sovereign independent state as hereinbefore defined shall be adopted and declared by the Parliament of the Union and that the South Africa Act 1909 (9 Edw. VII, c. 9) be amended accordingly;

And whereas it is expedient that the said Statute of Westminster, in so far as its provisions are applicable to the Union of South Africa, and an Afrikaans version thereof, shall be adopted as an Act of Parliament of the Union of South Africa;

Section 2 reads:

The Parliament of the Union shall be the sovereign legislative power in and over the Union, and notwithstanding anything in any other law contained, no Act of the Parliament of the United Kingdom and Northern Ireland [*sic*] passed after the eleventh day of December, 1931, shall extend, or be deemed to extend, to the Union as part of the law of the Union, unless extended thereto by an Act of the Parliament of the Union.

Section 3 provides that the sections of the Statute of Westminster applying to the Union[2] (and its preamble) 'shall be deemed to be an

---

[1] No. 69 of 1934. Printed in Kennedy and Schlosberg, *The Law and Custom of the South African Constitution*, p. 614.

[2] Sections 1, 2, 3, 4, 5, 6, 11, and 12.

Act of the Parliament of the Union, and shall be construed accordingly'.[1]

In the preamble (whose force is, of course, only expository, not legal) there is one clear error of statement, the second recital. The Statute of Westminster did not ratify, confirm, and establish *all* the resolutions and declarations set forth in the reports of the 1926 and 1930 Conferences in so far as they required legislation by the Imperial Parliament, but only *certain* of them, as the preamble to the Statute itself accurately recites.[2] The recital in the Act follows the minor heresy mentioned above. Otherwise, the preamble is unexceptionable. Indeed, it is quite unusually unexceptionable, for it is equally consistent with the orthodox view of the law and with the major heresy. Even the striking declaration that South Africa is a 'sovereign independent state' has the disarming qualification 'as hereinbefore defined', a reference to the sentence quoted from the Balfour Memorandum.

It may even be doubted whether the first clause of section 2, which is generally regarded in orthodox circles as going beyond the Statute of Westminster,[3] necessarily does so. Of course, the establishment of a sovereign coequal with the Imperial Parliament is clearly neither achieved nor authorized by the Statute of Westminster. But the equation of sovereign independence with 1926 Dominion status in the preamble, coupled with the provision now to be found in section 1 of the South Africa Act[4] that 'the people of the Union humbly acknowledge the sovereignty of Almighty God', strongly suggest that in South Africa sovereignty is less a term of art than a complimentary expression.[5] The second part of the section, however, does go beyond the restriction of the power of the Imperial Parliament effected by section 4 of the Statute of Westminster[6] in requiring subsequent extension of an Imperial Act to the Union by the Union Parliament as well as prior request and consent by the Union Government.

[1] The remaining sections of the Act, though important, do not touch the issues here discussed.

[2] The preamble to the statute is printed in the Schedule to the Act. (This does not appear from Kennedy and Schlosberg's reprint.) Thus the Act contradicts itself upon its face.

[3] e.g. Professor A. B. Keith, in 16 *Journ. Comp. Leg.* 290.

[4] Inserted by the South Africa Act Amendment Act, No. 9 of 1925.

[5] Compare the dissenting judgment of Kennedy C.J. in *State (Ryan)* v. *Lennon*, [1935] I. R. 170, 204–5 (below, p. 538, n. 7) where legal effect is attributed to a similar acknowledgement.

[6] 'No Act of Parliament of the United Kingdom passed after the commencement of this Act shall extend, or be deemed to extend, to a Dominion as part of the law of that Dominion, unless it is expressly declared in that Act that that Dominion has requested, and consented to, the enactment thereof.'

To the extent to which the Act does go beyond the Statute, whether in its enactment of sovereign independence or in its restriction of the legislative authority of the Imperial Parliament, it is, of course, from the orthodox point of view, invalid. But from the orthodox point of view the remarkable feature of the Act is not that one or two of its provisions may be slightly *ultra vires*, but that some parts of it are utterly otiose, serving no conceivable purpose. Why does the preamble declare it 'expedient' that the status of South Africa, already (according to its own recital) established in law by the Statute of Westminster, should be 'adopted and declared' over again by the Union Parliament, and that the Statute should be re-enacted in the Union? What meaning can attach to section 3 of the Act? If the Statute is law in the Union, it is law, and no amount of repetition will make it more so.

But the legislature of a nation of jurists cannot have intended such elaborate futility. Consideration of the political background supplies a clue: construed by the canons, not of orthodoxy, but of either of the heresies above mentioned, the otiose provisions become significant. The Act must have been intended to be construed by these canons. Without offending against imperial theory, or offending as little as possible, it nevertheless proceeds on the assumption that not the imperial, but the nationalist theory is true. It only requires the re-enactment of the South Africa Act by the Union Parliament (odd imperial references have already been cleared out of its text),[1] and there will be no need to look beyond the Union statute-book for the whole of the written constitutional law of the Union.[2] The Status of the Union Act is an invitation to the South African courts to assert a local root for South African law and jurisdiction in place of the Imperial one.

Will the courts comply? No case since the Act has raised issues which compel a choice of *Grundnorm*, and until South African and British legislation clearly conflict on a practical point, the issue will not arise.[3] But if it should arise in the near future, it is difficult to

[1] By sections 5, 6, 7, 8, 9, 11 of the Status of the Union Act.

[2] Except the appeal by special leave to the Privy Council.

[3] Since this was written, His Majesty King Edward VIII's Declaration of Abdication Bill has been introduced into the Union parliament (January 1937). This bill assumes (and, for South Africa, authoritatively declares) a different view of the law concerning the abdication of a monarch than that taken by the Law Officers in the United Kingdom and implied in His Majesty's Declaration of Abdication Act, 1936, of the United Kingdom Parliament. But the South African Bill has indemnity clauses retrospectively validating acts done in the Union on either view of the law. It amounts, therefore, to another legislative assertion of the separateness of the South African from the Imperial legal system, but stops short of submitting the matter to the arbitrament of the courts.

predict what answer the courts will give. They are not the blind servants of the legislature; they are the servants of the law.[1] It is true that, as the authors of the leading text-book point out,[2] the South Africa Act does not 'vest' the judicial power in them, as the Australian Commonwealth Constitution does in its courts. But neither does the British North America Act in the Canadian courts, yet they exercise the power of judicial review.[3] The South African courts may well feel it their duty to maintain the Imperial *Grundnorm*, either by construing the Status of the Union Act narrowly or by holding some of it invalid. On the other hand, public opinion, the wish of the legislature, and local loyalty will tell in the opposite direction. The legislature might indirectly assist that tendency by requiring an oath of unequivocal local allegiance from newly appointed judges.[4]

The separate South African *Grundnorm*, if it comes to be established, may look to the Balfour Report or merely to the Status of the Union Act for the root of title of South African law. Or it may set up a fiction that the Statute of Westminster was a complete and irrevocable abdication of the power of the Imperial Parliament. In any case, it will do violence to law or to history, probably to both. But it may well be politically fortunate. There is much to be said for stealth and subtlety as methods of revolution,[5] if revolution there must be.

In Ireland we find for the first time an interest in the formal derivation of law for its own sake. The comparatively sophisticated utterances of intellectual revolutionaries[6] demand not merely freedom, but freedom springing from an Irish source, and the factious populace expresses the same thought when it paints on the walls of Dublin 'Damn your concessions, England!' The *Grundnorm* has

[1] Dr. van Themaat, in 53 *S.A.L.J.* 50, surely goes too far in assuming that the South African courts are 'subjected' (*onderworpe*) to the Union Parliament. For his general view see 15 *Journ. Comp. Leg.* 47.

[2] Kennedy and Schlosberg, *Law and Custom of the South African Constitution*, p. 87.

[3] For a suggestive discussion of the rivalry between the principle of parliamentary sovereignty and the principle of the supremacy of the law, see Mr. Justice Dixon in 51 *L.Q.R.* 590.

[4] The oath required of members of Parliament by s. 51 of the South Africa Act as amended by s. 7 of the Status of the Union Act is equivocal between imperial and local allegiance.

[5] Establishment of a separate *Grundnorm* in any of these senses would enable legislation for secession to be validly passed. There would remain the practical problem of securing the consent of the King as a member of the legislature. This problem is dealt with by s. 4 of the *Status of the Union Act* and by the *Royal Executive Functions and Seals Act* 1934 (No. 70 of 1934). See below, p. 590.

[6] e.g. T. MacSwiney, *Principles of Freedom* (Dublin, 1921), ch. xvii.

descended into the market-place. The abortive proclamation of Easter 1916 did not demand any alteration of British law. It repudiated it entirely, asserting in its stead native Irish right,[1] and it was on the basis of this proclamation that the rebels fought, off and on, until the truce of 1921.[2]

The treaty settlement of 1921–2 was a compromise which simultaneously satisfied the British Government that the twenty-six counties were receiving their freedom at the hands of the Imperial Parliament, and satisfied the majority of the rebels that they had won it for themselves. In the negotiations each side gave up something. The Irish representatives did not, as they would have liked, claim retrospective recognition in the new Constitution of the authority of the revolutionary Dáils, but contented themselves with making ratification by the existing Dáil under another name a condition precedent to the operation of the Constitution. The British delegates, satisfied on pure doctrinal grounds that the authority of the new Free State could have no derivation but from the Imperial Parliament, did not insist upon explicit recognition of this, and allowed the dangerous Article 2 to go into the Constitution.[3]

Controversy concerning the circumstances and meaning of the Treaty Settlement is endless and absorbing. Some account of it is given above.[4] From the lawyer's point of view, however, it is wholly inconclusive. We shall, therefore, in the best English and Irish tradition, confine this discussion to decided cases.

Until 1924 the judicial system operating in Southern Ireland under the Government of Ireland Act, 1920,[5] served, by virtue of Article 75 of the Constitution, as the judicial system of the Free State.[6] Upon the establishment of the Free State the judges of the existing courts

---

[1] 'We declare the right of the people of Ireland to the Ownership of Ireland, and to the unfettered control of Irish destinies, to be sovereign and indefeasible. The long usurpation of that right by a foreign power and government has not extinguished the right, nor can it ever be extinguished except by the destruction of the people.'

[2] See above, Chapter III, section iii.

[3] 'All powers of government and all authority legislative, executive, and judicial in Ireland, are derived from the people of Ireland and the same shall be exercised in the Irish Free State (Saorstát Éireann) through the organizations established by or under, and in accord with, this Constitution.'

[4] Chapter III, section iii. See Pakenham, *Peace by Ordeal*, and Mansergh, *The Irish Free State; its Government and Politics*. For an analytical jurist's view, Kohn, *The Constitution of the Irish Free State*, ch. vi.

[5] Except the Court of Appeal for All Ireland.

[6] The form of Art. 75 (like Art. 73, which continued the existing general law until amended) was not a saving of the existing situation so that it continued *suo proprio vigore*, but an adoption of the *de facto* situation existing at the time of coming into force of the Constitution, without reference to its origins: *R. (Armstrong)* v. *County Court Judge of Wicklow*, [1924] 2 I.R. 139.

were continued in office without reappointment, but judges of superior courts were given an opportunity of resigning. The majority did not resign. Accordingly for the first two years of the Free State the courts consisted preponderantly of men who had personally accepted the British allegiance during the Troubles. Naturally in the circumstances, these courts were chary of pronouncing authoritatively upon the fundamentals of the Free State Constitution; and in fact there was no case where the question of the ultimate formal source of Free State law came up clearly for decision. There are some equivocal *obiter dicta* of which the most that can be said is that they do not preclude the idea that the Treaty, the Constitution, and the Constituent Act, or some or one of them, may amount to a constitutional novation.[1] One point, however, was clearly decided: the acts of the first Dáil and its instrumentalities are, from the Free State point of view, not only void but illegal.[2] There is no constitutional continuity between the revolutionary Dáils and the Free State.[3]

The majority of the members of the permanent judicature constituted in 1924[4] were newly appointed.[5] A new confidence, and a willingness to pronounce upon ultimate questions even when they were not strictly in issue, were immediately apparent. Thus Meredith, J., in 1925 said that the 'Constitution must be recognized by the Courts as an original source of jurisdiction, and, as regards the whole code of law to be applied, it is the one and only root of title'.[6] A *dictum* of Kennedy, C.J., (with which, however, the rest of the Court did not associate itself) in *in re Reade*[7] suggests that in his view the Treaty rather than the Constitution is the beginning of the Free State; but it seems not to be intended to cover more than the question of valid state succession, which does not necessarily amount to constitutional

---

[1] *R. (Childers)* v. *Adjutant General*, [1923] 1 I.R. 5, 14 (on the Provisional Government of 1922); *R. (O'Connell)* v. *Military Governor*, [1924] 2 I.R. 104; *R. (Armstrong)* v. *County Court Judge of Wicklow*, [1924] 2 I.R. 139, 144, 146, 151, 153.

[2] *R. (Kelly)* v. *Maguire and O'Sheil*, [1923] 2 I.R. 58.

[3] The Dáil Courts and Instrumentalities Winding-Up Act, 1923, provided for the appointment of a Commissioner with a wide discretion to settle questions arising out of the jurisdiction of the former Dáil courts. The tendency of the Act was to save their judgements as far as possible. But though it treats them tenderly, it is clear that any force they may continue to have is *conferred*, not merely *recognized*, by the Act.

[4] Under the Courts of Justice Act, No. 10 of 1924. Mr. Justice Hanna writes of the new judicial system: 'It effectively secures the complete disruption of the system of British Courts in the Saorstát.' (*The Statutes of the Irish Free State, 1922 to 1928*, p. 18.) It is difficult to see what this can mean, beyond the mere fact that the existing Acts were repealed, for the new system is British in all respects except the method and extent of its decentralization.

[5] Two judges from the former courts were appointed to the new courts; there were seven new appointments.

[6] *Cahill* v. *Attorney-General*, [1925] 1 I.R. 70.   [7] [1927] I.R. 31, 49.

continuity.[1] Subsequent dicta of the Chief Justice confirm this view;
thus, in *Lynam* v. *Butler* (*No. 2*)[2] he refers to 'the Constitution, the
Bunreacht, or fundamental structure upon which the State was set
by the Dáil sitting as a Constituent Assembly', a description which
he repeats in his dissenting judgment in the great case of *State
(Ryan)* v. *Lennon*.[3] In the latter case Fitzgibbon, J., one of the
majority in the Supreme Court, quoted with assent counsel's proposition that 'the Constituent Assembly proclaimed the Constitution by
virtue of its own supreme legislative authority'.[4]

A tendency to stress the element of popular sovereignty is exempli-
fied by an *obiter dictum* of Hanna, J., in *Carolan* v. *Minister of Defence*,[5]
that Article 2[6] 'established in law, not for the Saorstát alone, but
for Ireland, and in no metaphorical sense, the sovereignty of the
people of Ireland'.[7] In so far as this theory involves a presumption
in favour of the rigidity of the Constitution, it is decisively rejected
in *State (Ryan)* v. *Lennon*.[8] Meredith, J., in the High Court, is explicit
on this point:

'The Constitution itself is the exclusive source from which this Court
can derive any principle of law on the strength of which it has jurisdiction to declare any law to be invalid. Of course, to determine whether
any law contravenes the Constitution the Court has to analyse what is
contained in that law and what is contained in the Constitution, and
then to determine whether the law is consistent with the Constitution;
and this reasoning may, and indeed must, follow principles of construction. But these principles are not principles of law constituting part of
the subject matter of the comparison involved in the question whether
a law is consistent with the Constitution. So it is true to say that there
are no principles of law in relation to which the validity of any law is to
be tested except those enshrined in the Constitution. Our common law
does not contain any principles of constitutional law, and Article 73

[1] In *Fogarty* v. *O'Donoghue*, [1926] I.R. 531 it was held by the Supreme Court that
the Free State was equally entitled to the funds of the Republican Dáil whether by
continuity of title or by mere *de facto* succession. It was accordingly unnecessary to
decide by which right it held.
[2] [1933] I.R. 74, 94–5.   [3] [1935] I.R. 170, 203.
[4] [1935] I.R. 170, 225.   [5] [1927] I.R. 62, 70.
[6] 'Subject to this Constitution and to the extent to which they are not inconsistent
therewith, the laws in force in the Irish Free State (Saorstát Éireann) at the date of
the coming into operation of this Constitution shall continue to be of full force and
effect until the same or any of them shall have been repealed or amended by enactment of the Oireachtas.'
[7] If this 'sovereignty of the people' is recognized as the ground of the validity of
the power of the Third Dáil and therefore of the Constituent Act, it is relevant to the
Grundnorm, and Article 2 is merely declaratory. If, on the other hand, it is merely
enacted by Article 2 for the first time, it is irrelevant to the *Grundnorm*.
[8] [1935] I.R. 170.

of the Constitution[1] did not enact by reference any principles of constitutional law, in relation to which any law could be held by this Court
to be valid or invalid.'[2]

This admirable exposition of the roots of Free State law is vitiated,
from the point of view of the present study, by the fact that in the
succeeding paragraph the learned judge makes it clear that his view
is based, not on considerations of the source of Free State law, but
on the limitations upon the Court's power of judicial review of legislation, which power he assumes to be conferred solely by Article 65.[3]
In view of *Marbury* v. *Madison*[4] and the prevalence of judicial review
throughout the British Empire, it seems preferable to regard Article
65 as in this respect merely declaratory. The other two judges of the
High Court did not find it necessary to consider fundamental questions, and concurred in the result with Meredith, J., as did Fitzgibbon, J.[5], and Murnaghan, J., who formed the majority of the
Supreme Court. Kennedy, C.J., in an interesting dissenting judgment, put forward the remarkable view that Acts of the Oireachtas[6]
inconsistent with the Natural Law are void.[7]

Article 73[8] has been uniformly interpreted not as simply suffering
the English law to continue, but as re-enacting as Free State law the
corpus of United Kingdom law in force in the Free State area at the
date of the Constitution.[9] On the other hand, it has not been ques-

---

[1] See below, n. 8.   [2] [1935] I.R. 170, 178–9.
[3] 'The judicial power of the High Court shall extend to the question of the validity
of any law having regard to the provisions of the Constitution. In all cases in which
such matters shall come into question, the High Court alone shall exercise original
jurisdiction.'
[4] (1803) 1 Cranch 137. This decision of the Supreme Court of the United States
established the right of that court to review legislation for conformity to the Constitution.
[5] A *dictum* in his judgment is cited above, p. 537.
[6] The Free State Legislature.
[7] From the acknowledgement in the preamble to the Constituent Act 'that all
lawful authority comes from God to the people', coupled with Article 2 of the Constitution, he argued that 'if any legislation of the Oireachtas (including any purported
amendment of the Constitution) were to offend against that acknowledged ultimate
Source from which the legislative authority has come through the people to the
Oireachtas, as, for instance, if it were repugnant to the Natural Law, such legislation
would be unconstitutional and invalid': [1935] I.R. 170, 204–5. The Constitution
(Amendment No. 17) Act, No. 37. of 1931, was, in the late Chief Justice's view, invalid
on this ground.
[8] 'Subject to this Constitution and to the extent to which they are not inconsistent
therewith, the laws in force in the Irish Free State (Saorstát Éireann) at the date of
the coming into operation of this constitution shall continue to be of full force and effect
until the same or any of them shall have been repealed or amended by enactment of
the Oireachtas.' This Article is omitted from Keith's reprint, in *Speeches and Documents on the British Dominions, 1918–1931.*
[9] *O'Callaghan* v. *O'Sullivan*, [1925] 1 I.R. 90; *London Finance and Discount*

tioned that the 'law in force' referred to in that article is the British law, and not such law as the revolutionary Dáils had enacted.

In the few appeals that came to the Privy Council from the Free State before 1935, it was not necessary to consider what was the basis of Free State law. In *Moore* v. *Attorney-General for the Irish Free State*[1] the question arose squarely. Its treatment by the Board is unsatisfactory,[2] possibly owing to the fact that the Free State Government, which did not recognize the jurisdiction, was not represented by counsel, but the conclusion is simple and clear:

> 'Thus the Treaty received the force of law, both in the United Kingdom and in Ireland, by reason of the passing of an Act of the Imperial Parliament; and the Constitutional Act owed its validity to the same authority.'[3]

According to the principles laid down in the Canadian case of *British Coal Corporation* v. *R.*,[4] which was heard concurrently, it would seem that, in deciding *Moore's Case*, the Judicial Committee regarded itself as in effect an Irish court, deciding a question of Irish law, not as an imperial, still less a United Kingdom court.[5] The *dictum* quoted is therefore in direct and immediate conflict with all shades of doctrine in the Irish courts on the same point. But since the substantial decision in *Moore's Case* was that the appeal from the Free State to the Privy Council had been effectively abolished by Irish legislation, there will be no opportunity for a continuation of the conflict. And since the dictum quoted is that of a court which by its own decision had already ceased to be a court superior to the Irish courts, it would hardly be binding authority in the Irish courts, even if they were otherwise prepared to defer to Privy Council decisions, which is by no means likely.

We are left, then, with a mass of dicta of the Free State courts, not obviously consistent with one another, and all in some measure *obiter*, as the best available evidence of the root of Irish Free State law. He would be a bold man who would attempt, on these authorities, to define the Irish *Grundnorm*. Since the establishment of the

---

Company v. *Butler*, [1929] I.R. 90. The opinion of the Board in *Performing Right Society* v. *Bray*, [1930] A.C. 377, 399, [1930] I.R. 509, 528, tends in the opposite direction; but Privy Council decisions are no longer authoritative in the Free State.

[1] [1935] A.C. 484; [1935] I.R. 472.

[2] See an acute criticism by Dr. W. I. Jennings, 52 *L.Q.R.* 183 sqq.

[3] [1935] A.C. 484, 492; [1935] I.R. 472, 479.   [4] [1935] A.C. 500, 520-1.

[5] Contrast *Wakely* v. *Triumph Cycle Co.*, [1924] 1 K.B. 214, where the King's Bench Division had to construe the Free State Constitution as a matter of British law. In fact, the same point, arising in Irish law, was decided, on the same premises, in the opposite sense by the High Court of the Free State in *Gieves Ltd.* v. *O'Connor*, [1924] 2 I.R. 182.

permanent judicature, however, they all point unequivocally to its separateness from the United Kingdom *Grundnorm*. Despite the lack of a decision directly in point, no reader of the Irish Reports can be left in any doubt about the matter. Counsel in the Free State do not even argue the other view. For the Irish Free State, then, the breach with the formal unity of Imperial law has been consummated.

A change of *Grundnorm* is, by definition, an event outside and prior to the law. It constitutes a technical revolution, for the *Grundnorm* embodies the identity of the State. In the light of subsequent developments, the foundation of the Irish Free State proves to have been an instance not of extreme devolution by the Imperial Parliament, but of revolution coupled with reconciliation on a contractual basis.[1] Retrospectively, that is, from the orthodox British point of view; but the Irish view, though vague in detail, has been consistent throughout in this essential respect, and has been justified in the event. For this reason the separation of the Irish *Grundnorm* has not imposed the same strain on the intellectual integrity of those responsible for it as will the South African attempt, if it is successful. It is one thing to insist that an admittedly catastrophic change amounts to a juristic revolution; it is quite another to set up retrospectively by enacted fiction a catastrophe which never took place—to claim to have effected a revolution by due process of law.

The extreme fundamental vagueness which has rendered possible the shifting of the *Grundnorm* in South Africa and in Ireland is an anomalous quality of imperial law. For, just as the existence of a system of law as a system involves the postulation of a *Grundnorm*, so the working of the system normally involves the rendering of that *Grundnorm* explicit. In the British Commonwealth two peculiar factors have operated to postpone the latter process. One is the empirical character of the case-law method. The other is the circumstance that, by reason of the archaic inflexibility of the general constitutional law of the Empire, the forces of constitutional controversy which should have hammered out a new legal system have operated instead in the alternative field of constitutional convention.

2. *A Common Jurisdiction*

Among the important institutions of the former centralized Empire which have survived into the co-operative Commonwealth, a judicial

---

[1] The contractual quality of the Treaty was in effect recognized by the decision in *Moore's Case*, [1935] A.C. 484, 499.

institution, the jurisdiction of the Privy Council, is the most vigorous in its daily operation and at the same time the most archaic in form. The common legislature has in the Statute of Westminster to the best of its ability divested itself of its imperial character, and is lapsing into comparative desuetude. In function, though not in dignity, the common titular executive is being split asunder. But the Judicial Committee still sits in Whitehall, drawing its authority from the same prerogative which the Norman kings had, and observing in its proceedings a Standing Order of 1627. A succession of nineteenth-century statutes regulated its personnel, but without drastic change. In the general tactful *bouleversement* of ancient imperial institutions in the twentieth century, it suffered only three losses, if losses they can be called: in 1900 a newly created jurisdiction which it might have expected to acquire was denied it;[1] in 1933 it lost one jurisdiction which it had never been anxious to exercise,[2] and another, recently assigned to it, which it had never consolidated.[3] Meanwhile its territory was steadily and almost automatically extending with every new acquisition of a dependency by the Crown.[4]

The comparative vitality of this institution is no accident, because the maxim 'Self-government is better than good government', upon which the emancipation of the overseas dominions has proceeded, by its nature applies last of all and with the least force to the judicial arm. Judicial power as exercised by superior courts does not, or should not, belong to government at all except in a marginal sense. On any theory the faculty of judgment is at least more absolute and universal and less varying according to person, place, and circumstances than administration and legislation. There are some nationalists who, counting the objectivity of the courts a major part of freedom, think themselves never so free as when that objectivity is best secured. They are even prepared to regard an appeal to an external court as an addition to freedom if it increases that security. There are others who hold that the form, traditions, and personnel of a nation's judicial institutions are properly regarded as products of its national genius, and it does not lie well in the mouths of Englishmen —whose own history is the strongest argument for this view—to deny it categorically, still less to construe it as a claim for the corrup-

---

[1] Certain kinds of constitutional cases from Australia. See below, pp. 548–9.

[2] Criminal appeals from Canada by Canadian Act 23 and 24 Geo. V, c. 53. See below, pp. 549–50.

[3] Irish Free State appeals by the Constitution (Amendment No. 22) Act, No. 45 of 1933. See below, pp. 549–50.

[4] The latest extension is to the territories put under mandate to Great Britain and the Dominions.

tion of justice. In fact, a court of law needs to be both objective and *sympathique*. It is legitimate for, say, Calvinists to stress the one quality, and Celts the other. This very difference can be seen in the views of Irishmen and South Africans. Thus the first President of the Irish Free State wrote in 1923 to the members of the committee which was to draw up a new scheme of judicature for Ireland:[1]

'In the long struggle for the right to rule our own country there has been no sphere of the administration lately ended which impressed itself on the minds of our people as a standing monument of alien government more than the system, the machinery and the administration of law and justice, which supplanted in comparatively modern times[2] the laws and institutions till then a part of the living national organism. . . .

'Thus it comes that there is nothing more prized among our newly won liberties than the liberty to construct a system of judiciary and an administration of law and justice according to the dictates of our own needs and after a pattern of our own designing.'

And a judge of the High Court of the Free State writes:[3]

'One of the most effective institutions, forged more as a weapon against British administration than as a definite and perfect system, was the Dáil Judiciary.'

(The Dáil Courts[4] at one stage refused to hear British cases cited, and relied for inspiration on natural justice, Roman law, the *Code Civil*, and old Irish law.) Even when discounted as heavily as utterances of their type must be, these statements reveal a view, sincerely held, which is radically opposed to that of, say, Dr. Manfred Nathan, who writes[5] that:

'the continued existence of appeals to the Judicial Committee . . . does not affect the independent status of the Dominions, any more than the status of any international state is affected by the Permanent Court of International Justice at The Hague. The final appeal to the Judicial Committee is not a mark of the sovereignty of the Crown, but a matter of convenience in that there should be a final court of resort for members of the Commonwealth.'

A more nationalist South African jurist, attacking the Privy Council appeal, does so on the purely abstract ground that the Judicial Com-

[1] Letter of President W. T. Cosgrave, quoted in Hanna, *The Statute Law of the Irish Free State, 1922 to 1928* (Dublin, Thorn, 1929), p. 17.
[2] The supplanting was completed in the reign of James I (R.T.E.L.).
[3] Hanna, op. cit., p. 30.
[4] i.e. the courts set up by the authority of the revolutionary Dáil. See above, pp. 117–18.   [5] *Empire Government* (1928), p. 91.

mittee cannot recognize the 'sovereignty' of South Africa.[1] To the Irish nationalist, then, judgment by alien judges, however upright, is alien government; to the South African nationalist, it is not necessarily so. Neither view is to be preferred to the other, for nationalism is not a creed of objective reason.

Even in countries which take a thoroughly objective view of law, there are gradations in the objectivity of the courts. In practice the judicial function can nowhere be kept logically pure. Courts of first instance, especially petty courts, must and do temper the logic of the law with personal understanding, based on knowledge of the background of their cases. The superior courts, especially the appellate courts, which deal with considerable questions of private law, are more faithful to the canons of pure reason, but even in them the general outlook of the judge and his habit of thought play a large conscious and a larger unconscious part. And those tribunals which, under rigid constitutions, are charged with the exalted duty of interpreting and enunciating fundamental law must, if they are not to wreck the constitutional organism, pay more heed to 'public policy'[2] than do the courts of private law.

It is upon no more rigid assumptions than these that we shall discuss the only common jurisdiction of the countries comprising the British Empire or Commonwealth. We shall seek to discover the significance of this common jurisdiction in relation first to the formal unity of the Commonwealth discussed in the last section, then to the three political programmes of imperial unity, nationalism, and provincialism, and finally to the general quality of law and justice throughout the Empire.

The first question, which links up with the preceding section, can be answered upon grounds of general theory, apart from the peculiar character of the Privy Council jurisdiction. No court will assign different ultimate roots to different portions of its jurisdiction, or (which is perhaps the same thing) to different parts of the law which it applies, unless explicitly directed to do so. That is to say, there is a strong tendency, amounting to a presumption, that any court will apply the same ultimate criteria of validity to all the law that it administers. Can this presumption ever be displaced? Is it possible

---

[1] Professor H. ver Loren van Themaat, 53 *S. Afr. Law Journ.*, p. 49, quoted below, p. 544.

[2] 'Public policy' is a phrase used by judges to explain decisions for which they are unable to cite strictly legal grounds. Some principles first tentatively enunciated as 'public policy', such as those governing contracts in restraint of trade, have by repeated judicial adoption become in effect rules of common law.

for a court to have two quite unconnected sources of jurisdiction, to administer two systems of law which are, in the formal sense described in the last section, unrelated ? Dr. van Themaat thinks not. Having asserted the formal separateness of the South African system of law, he writes:[1]

'What will the position then be if the British Parliament passes an act conflicting with section 4 of the Statute of Westminster, or amending or repealing any section of the Statute ? The Privy Council, being the servant of the British Parliament, will fully acknowledge and apply the act; our own courts will not acknowledge and apply it, since they are subjected to the Union Parliament. . . . The retention of the Privy Council appeal is accordingly inconsistent with the legal position of the Union of South Africa, as laid down in the Status of the Union Act 1934.'

The assumption seems to be that a court can administer only that system of law to which the legislature constituting it belongs;[2] it must accept as its sole criteria of validity those of that system. But the present jurisdiction of the Appellate Division of the Supreme Court of South Africa itself demands a gloss upon this view, if indeed it does not refute it. The Appellate Division is constituted by South African law. Appeals lie to it also from the Supreme Court of Southern Rhodesia.[3] But Southern Rhodesia is unquestionably under the authority of the British Parliament, and belongs therefore to that British system of law from which Dr. van Themaat assumes that the South African system is separate. Therefore the Appellate Division derives its jurisdiction from two separate roots, and administers two formally independent systems of law.[4] The conclusion seems to

---

[1] 53 *S. Afr. Law Journ.* 49, 51. I am indebted to Sir de V. Graaff for assistance in the translation.

[2] The cruder and more obvious implication, that courts are always 'subjected' to legislatures, would preclude the possibility of judicial review, and so cannot be intended. For an exposition of Dr. van Themaat's view of the relation of courts to legislatures see his article, 15 *Journ. Comp. Leg.* 47.

[3] By Act No. 14 of 1931 of Southern Rhodesia, and Act No. 18 of 1931 of the Union.

[4] There is an interesting, though not complete, analogy in the position of Australian State courts which enjoy both federal and State jurisdictions. There is often great ambiguity whether a court is exercising federal or State jurisdiction, or both simultaneously. They are not in theory incommensurable, since the authority of both is derived from imperial legislation; but in fact they may prove to be so, since from State jurisdiction an optional appeal lies to the Privy Council, while the federal parliament has confined appeals from federal jurisdiction to the High Court, and the Privy Council and the High Court seem to take different views both of the validity of that federal legislation and of the distinction between State and federal jurisdiction. See Report of the Royal Commission on the Constitution of the Commonwealth (1929), pp. 108–10; J. G. Latham, *Australia and the British Commonwealth* (Macmillan, 1929), pp. 116–17.

be that if the laws of two systems concur in conferring jurisdictions in both systems upon a court (or if those laws reciprocally confer and permit the conferment of both jurisdictions), the court may exercise both jurisdictions. It may even, upon identical data which are significant in both systems, but in relation to which the provisions of their laws differ, reach different conclusions in its two jurisdictions. But if a conflict should arise through failure of the laws conferring jurisdiction to coincide, or through one system purporting to lay down criteria of validity for the other system different from the criteria which that other system itself accepts, the court will have to abandon one or other allegiance. In choosing, it will naturally adhere to the system by whose law it is actually constituted, upon which its very existence as a tribunal depends. If it is constituted equally by both, its choice will be free.

It appears, accordingly, that a common jurisdiction can be shared by formally separate systems of law without their merging, but only if the provisions setting up the common jurisdiction in each system are concurrent and clearly defined. If such definition is lacking, and the common jurisdiction is constantly exercised, the court will tend to apply the same criteria of validity over the whole range of its jurisdiction, which may destroy the separateness of the systems.[1] If, however, the jurisdiction is only rarely exercised in one or other system, it may not have that effect. It is only because the Judicial Committee is slow to entertain appeals from South Africa,[2] and that its jurisdiction for the Free State, while it lasted, was as far as possible boycotted and frustrated,[3] that the phenomena described in the last section have been possible.

Before the second and third questions can be answered, it is necessary to describe the constitution and jurisdiction of the Judicial Committee, to ascertain the extent and manner in which its jurisdiction may be controlled by the Dominions, and to compare the Judicial Committee in a general way with other courts of law.

Some account has been given in the first section of this chapter of

---

[1] A court which in different parts of its jurisdiction has to apply different kinds of law *in pari materia* (whether or not those kinds of law belong to formerly separate systems) is under a strong temptation to decide that both laws say the same thing, thus saving itself from having to draw the line between the jurisdictions. Cf. *Smith* v. *Davis*, [1878] Buch. (S. Afr.) 66 (for which reference the writer is indebted to Professor R. W. Lee) and the numerous Scotch appeals which the House of Lords has decided on English law without inquiring too carefully whether or not Scots law is identical on the point, e.g., *McAlister (or Donoghue)* v. *Stevenson*, [1932] A.C. 562.
[2] See below, p. 553.
[3] See Hughes, *Judicial Autonomy in the British Commonwealth of Nations*.

the origin and early history of the Privy Council jurisdiction.[1] The Judicial Committee Act, 1833, and its successors did no more than constitute a committee of the Privy Council to which all petitions to His Majesty in Council in the nature of judicial appeals must be referred. Where an ordinary court gives a judgment of its own authority, the Judicial Committee merely advises the King in Council to make an order, though that order is in fact always made. The source of the Privy Council's jurisdiction is accordingly still the royal prerogative. Signs of the administrative origin of the tribunal appear in these and other peculiar formalities, and in the rule that the opinion of the Board is embodied in a single judgment, from which no dissent is expressed. This practice is imposed by an Order in Council of 1627, which is still in force, prescribing that,

> 'In voting of any cause, the lowest councillor is to speak first, and so it is to be carried by most voices; because every councillor hath equal vote there: and when the business is carried according to most voices, no publication is afterwards to be made, by any man, how the particular voices and opinions went.'[2]

But the Judicial Committee is now as scrupulously and purely judicial as any court in the Empire.[3]

By the Act of 1833 and later Acts, the Judicial Committee consists of the President of the Council, the Lord Chancellor of England, ex-Lords President, ex-Lord Chancellors, and all Privy Councillors who are or have been Lords of Appeal in Ordinary, judges of the Supreme Courts of England or Northern Ireland, of the Court of Session in Scotland, of the Supreme Court of Canada, the High Court of Australia, the Supreme Court of South Africa, or the Supreme Court of Newfoundland, or the superior courts in New Zealand, the Canadian provinces, or the Australian states, or who are or have been Chief Justices or Judges of a High Court in India (but not more than two of this class at the same time) together with others specially appointed up to the number of four, of whom two must be specially qualified in Indian law. The laymen, if there are any (Lords President are usually laymen), do not sit. The quorum is three. Indian and colonial appeals, except a few of great importance, are heard by boards of three. The majority of Dominion appeals are now heard by boards of five.[4] The Lord Chancellor determines what members shall hear what appeals by issuing invitations to sit.

[1] Above, pp. 519–20.
[2] Printed in Safford and Wheeler, *Privy Council Practice*, p. 133.
[3] The contrary view dies hard in Canada. Cf. Ollivier, *Le Canada, pays souverain?* (Montreal, 1935), pp. 186–8.   [4] See Note I, below, p. 574.

The law lords (i.e. the Lord Chancellor, ex-Lord Chancellors, and the Lords of Appeal in Ordinary) form the backbone of the committee. The board of three for Indian appeals normally consists of a law lord, one of the specially appointed members for India (who may be Indian or Anglo-Indian), and one other from any category. Boards of five have three or four law lords. Ex-judges of English and Scottish courts are often brought in, especially when business is heavy. Scottish law lords do more than their proportionate share in the Privy Council: their presence is especially valuable in appeals from Roman Law countries such as Quebec, South Africa, and Ceylon, and their knowledge of comparative law fortifies the tribunal in dealing with other systems alien to the Common Law. Dominion chief justices and some Dominion puisne judges are usually sworn of the Privy Council and, when in England, are asked to sit; but this happens so rarely that they are a negligible element in its constitution.[1] No Irish Free State judge has sat.

There are usually two divisions sitting during term, but three divisions have, on occasion, sat simultaneously. Sittings are on four days a week only, in the Treasury building at the corner of Downing Street and Whitehall. Members of the Board do not wear robes, though counsel do. This practice, and the circumstance that there is no dais, lend the tribunal an air of comparative intimacy and informality. The right of audience is enjoyed by English barristers and Scottish advocates, and by members of the bar of any tribunal from which an appeal lies to the Privy Council.[2]

In addition to its appellate jurisdiction from the overseas Empire and under the Foreign Jurisdiction Act, the Judicial Committee has odd scraps of jurisdiction within the United Kingdom,[3] and hears appeals from the Channel Islands[4] and the Isle of Man. It has also jurisdiction to decide matters referred to it by Order in Council of the United Kingdom.[5] The most important matter which has hither-

[1] For statistics of the composition of recent boards see Notes III and IV, below, pp. 575–6.

[2] Safford and Wheeler, *Privy Council Practice*, p. 135, n. (*e*). Members of another overseas Bar than that from which the actual appeal comes have been heard by the board in recent years. So the writer is informed by Mr. W. A. Barton.

[3] It hears appeals from certain Admiralty courts, from all ecclesiastical courts, and from the Joint Exchequer Board of Great Britain and Northern Ireland. It determines on special reference constitutional questions affecting Northern Ireland, and exercises quasi-judicial powers in certain ecclesiastical matters, in hearing persons aggrieved under schemes for endowed schools, and in licensing republication of books after the death of the author.

[4] The jurisdiction of the Privy Council over the Channel Islands was the forerunner and prototype of its modern imperial jurisdiction: Holdsworth, *History of English Law*, vol. i, pp. 520, 599.   [5] 43 T.L.R. 289.

to been so referred is the Labrador Boundary Question between Canada and Newfoundland, in 1927.

Overseas appeals come to the Judicial Committee in two ways: as of right, and by special leave of the Judicial Committee itself. Appeals as of right exist only where a right of appeal in prescribed categories of cases has been specially created by statute, letters patent, Order in Council, or otherwise. The instrument creating the right of appeal usually entrusts to the court appealed from the duty of granting or refusing leave to appeal in accordance with its terms. If that court refuses leave to appeal as of right, the applicant may apply to the Judicial Committee itself for special leave to appeal. Where a colonial or Dominion legislature has power to regulate courts of justice, that power, apart from local constitutional provisions, probably includes the power to restrict or prohibit appeals as of right.[1] An enactment that the judgment of a local court shall be 'final and conclusive' is sufficient to prohibit such appeals.[2]

When leave to appeal to the King in Council is given not by another court under the terms of a grant, but by the Judicial Committee itself in its discretion, it is called special leave to appeal.[3] The right to apply for special leave to appeal is, as we have already shown,[4] in its nature a right coextensive with British sovereignty, extending equally to territories which themselves have common law systems and to those under other kinds of law. It has always been regarded as a right closely related to the imperial prerogative of the Crown and not a matter of local law, so that before the Statute of Westminster legislation of a dominion or colony prohibiting application to the Privy Council for special leave to appeal was invalid[5] in the absence of an express power to legislate to that end given by an Imperial Act. Such power was given to the parliament of South Africa,[6] and, in respect only of appeals from the High Court, to the parliament of the

---

[1] It was so assumed by all parties in *Nadan* v. *R.* [1926] A.C. 482. But the correctness of the assumption is questioned by Mr. Justice Dixon in 10 *Aust. Law Journ.*, *Supp.*, pp. 102–3.

[2] Appeals still lie as of right from the courts of Australian states, Canadian provinces, and New Zealand; but not from the Supreme Court of Canada, the High Court of Australia, or any South African Court. Appeals from the Colonies and India normally come as of right.

[3] Special leave to appeal may be sought not only where there is no appeal as of right from the court below, but also after the court below has refused leave to appeal as of right, and may be granted either on the ground that the refusal was wrong, or on the ground that the matter ought in any case to be determined by His Majesty in Council.

[4] Above, p. 520.

[5] *Cushing* v. *Dupuy* (1880) 5 App. Cas. 409; *Nadan* v. *R.*, [1926] A.C. 482.

[6] South Africa Act, 1909, s. 106.

Commonwealth of Australia,[1] subject in each case to 'reservation' of the abolishing Act for the royal assent. No legislation has been passed under either of these powers. But the Commonwealth Constitution itself forbids appeals from the High Court,

> 'upon any question, howsoever arising, as to the limits *inter se* of the Constitutional powers of the Commonwealth and those of any State or States, or as to the limits *inter se* of the Constitutional powers of any two or more States, unless the High Court shall certify that the question is one which ought to be determined by Her Majesty in Council.'[2]

The High Court has only once granted such a certificate, and will be slow to grant another.[3]

At the Imperial Conference of 1926 the law regarding the competence of the Dominions to bar appeals to the Privy Council suffered no change, since resolutions of a conference do not change law. But constitutional conventions were then declared which radically enlarge the actual powers of the Dominions in this respect. In the first place, the efficacy of the reservation of bills was destroyed by the establishment of the rule that, in consenting or refusing his consent to a reserved bill, the King acts on the advice of Dominion ministers. In the second place, it was declared that—

> 'it was no part of the policy of His Majesty's Government in Great Britain that questions affecting judicial appeals should be determined otherwise than in accordance with the wishes of the part of the Empire primarily affected.'

This admission sets up, in effect, a convention that the Imperial Parliament will, at the request of a Dominion, abolish or limit the jurisdiction of the Privy Council for the Dominion. In the federal Dominions (Canada and Australia) the views of the provinces and states would have to be taken into consideration, to the extent hereinafter explained.[4]

To this political emancipation a large measure of legal emancipation was added by the Statute of Westminster, 1931. In the leading cases of *Moore* v. *Attorney-General for the Irish Free State*[5] and *British*

---

[1] Constitution, s. 74. But appeals direct to the Privy Council from state courts in matters concerning the interpretation of the Constitution (whether '*inter se* questions' or not) have been in fact prevented by making the investment of the state courts with jurisdiction in such matters conditional upon there being no appeal save to the High Court: Judiciary Act 1903–7, ss. 39, 39B, 40, 40A. There is, however, some doubt of the effectiveness of this legislation, arising from the distinction between State and Federal jurisdiction. See above, p. 544, n. 4.

[2] Constitution, s. 74.   [3] See below, pp. 565–7.   [4] See below, pp. 550, 551.

[5] [1935] A.C. 484, [1934] I.R. 472, upholding the Constitution (Amendment No. 22) Act 1933 of the Free State.

Coal Corporation v. *R.*[1] the Judicial Committee, interpreting section 2 of the Statute broadly, held that, by acts passed in 1933 under the powers expressed by the Statute, the Oireachtas had validly abolished all appeals from the Free State, and the Canadian parliament all criminal appeals from Canada.[2]

We shall now consider for each Dominion in turn what is the present extent in law of the appeal to the Privy Council by special leave, and what are the steps, if any, which each Dominion now has the power in law or convention to take for its abolition or limitation. It must not be thought that within the limits to be stated the Privy Council will, like an ordinary appellate court, hear any and every reasonable appeal. As will be explained below,[3] the board restricts narrowly, and in different measure for different Dominions, the class of cases in which it will grant special leave to appeal. But these are restrictions of discretion, not restrictions of law, and the Dominions have no certain guarantee of their continuance.

In Canada appeals lie both from the Supreme Court of Canada and from the highest courts of the provinces. Criminal law being a subject assigned to the federal legislature,[4] that legislature has, as we have seen, validly abolished appeals in criminal matters from all courts in Canada.[5] Property and civil rights, and procedure in civil matters in provincial courts, are, however, provincial subjects.[6] In view of section 8 of the Statute of Westminster, it seems clear that the federal legislature alone could not eliminate the right of appeal in civil matters, but that with the concurrence of the provincial legislatures it might. How much the provincial legislatures alone could achieve in this direction is doubtful. An alternative and a surer method of abolishing or further limiting appeals would be a request to the United Kingdom Government to promote legislation in the imperial parliament. Under the 1926 Report, the government and parliament would be bound in convention to accede to such a request. But the request would, by reason of the conventions governing amendments of the British North America Act, require to be made by the provinces as well as the Dominion. It is to be noted that, since constitutional issues may arise in criminal cases, the Supreme Court

---

[1] [1935] A.C. 500, upholding Canadian Act 23 and 24 Geo. V, c. 53.
[2] See, for comment on these decisions, W. I. Jennings in 52 *L.Q.R.* 173, V. C. Macdonald in 13 *Can. Bar Rev.* 625, and Mr. Justice Dixon in 10 *Aust. Law Journ.*, *Supp.* 96.
[3] Pp. 552–4.   [4] British North America Act, s. 91.
[5] Canadian Act 23–4 Geo. V, c. 53; *British Coal Corporation* v. *R.* [1935] A.C. 500.
[6] British North America Act, s. 92.

of Canada has now for the first time an opportunity to determine some constitutional matters finally, without the possibility of further appeal.[1]

In Australia, as we have seen, there is already in that preponderant number of constitutional cases which raise '*inter se* questions' no appeal to the Privy Council except by certificate of the High Court, which is now never granted.[2] In the residue of constitutional cases,[3] and in all other cases, an appeal by special leave lies from both Commonwealth and state courts.[4] The Statute of Westminster does not apply to Australia until adopted.[5] It might not appear at first sight that its adoption would confer any additional power to abolish or restrict the Privy Council appeal, since the Commonwealth parliament has already under the Constitution power to limit the appeal from the High Court and from state courts in matters of federal jurisdiction, and the Statute does not apply to, and cannot be adopted by, the States. It is probable, however, that, in view of the decision in *British Coal Corporation* v. *R.*[6] and the narrow terms of section 9 (1) of the Statute, it will give power to the Commonwealth parliament to abolish the appeals as of right and by special leave from state courts in matters of state jurisdiction.[7] In any case, those appeals can be abolished by constitutional amendment according to the prescribed procedure by referendum[8] or by imperial legislation requested by the Commonwealth and the states.

---

[1] The validity of legislation creating criminal offences can nevertheless still be considered by the Privy Council by way of appeal from an advisory opinion of the Supreme Court, as in *in re Section 498A of the Criminal Code, The Times*, 29 January, 1937, [1937] W.N. 56. But since the Supreme Court only gives advisory opinions on questions referred to it by Order in Council of the Dominion, the Dominion government could prevent such a question going to the Privy Council by raising it instead in the form of a test prosecution.

[2] Constitution, s. 74. See below, p. 567.

[3] i.e. cases concerning the interpretation of the Constitution, but not of those sections of it directly concerned with the distribution of powers among Commonwealth and states: e.g. *Shell Co. of Australia* v. *Federal Commission of Taxation*, [1931] A.C. 275 (whether vesting of judicial power in executive is permissible), and *James* v. *Commonwealth*, [1936] A.C. 578 (whether Commonwealth may infringe freedom of interstate trade). And, of course, cases concerning State constitutions, e.g. *McCawley* v. *R.* [1920] A.C. 691: *Attorney-General for New South Wales* v. *Trethowan*, [1932] A.C. 526. See below, pp. 566–7.

[4] Except in so far as appeals on constitutional questions from state courts direct to the Privy Council have been circumvented by the legislative device mentioned above, p. 549, n. 1.

[5] The Federal Attorney-General has announced the Commonwealth Government's intention of introducing legislation for the adoption of the Statute; 10 *Aust. Law Journ., Supp.* 108.

[6] [1935] A.C. 500.

[7] See Mr. Justice Dixon in 10 *Aust. Law Journ., Supp.*, at p. 101.

[8] Constitution, s. 128.

The South African Parliament, having already in effect full power under the South Africa Act[1] to abolish or limit Privy Council appeals, had nothing more to gain under the Statute of Westminster.[2]

The New Zealand Parliament cannot apart from the Statute of Westminster limit the appeal by special leave. If it adopted the Statute it would probably, despite section 8 of the Statute, have complete freedom in this respect.

There is now no appeal from the Irish Free State.[3]

It remains to consider the habitual limitations which the Judicial Committee has imposed upon itself by declaring the principles upon which it will grant special leave to appeal. In settling these limits, successive boards have frankly taken into consideration the advance of Dominion status and the different shades of opinion regarding the Privy Council appeal which prevail in different Dominions. In 1882, in *Prince* v. *Gagnon*,[4] the Board stated:

> 'Their Lordships are not prepared to advise Her Majesty to exercise her prerogative by admitting an appeal to Her Majesty in Council from the Supreme Court of a Dominion, save where the case is of gravity involving some matter of public interest or some important question of law, or affecting property of considerable amount, or where the case is otherwise of some public importance or of a very substantial character.'[5]

This rule was afterwards further strengthened by pronouncements that even cases coming within these limits would not be heard if the decision of the court below was clearly right in law,[6] and that where the appellant had already chosen to appeal to the Dominion Supreme Court rather than to the Privy Council, leave to appeal from the Supreme Court to the Privy Council should only be granted 'under special circumstances'.[7] Nor will the board entertain questions, of whatever public importance, which are not, or have ceased to be, practical issues.[8] Distinctions between one Dominion and another

---

[1] s. 106.

[2] See above, pp. 548–9.

[3] *Moore* v. *Attorney-General for the Irish Free State*, [1935] A.C. 484, [1934] I.R. 472.

[4] 8 App. Cas. 103, 105.

[5] The same rule was applied to Australian appeals in *Daily Telegraph* v. *McLaughlin*, [1904] A.C. 776.

[6] *Cité de Montreal* v. *Ecclésiastiques de St. Sulpice*, 14 App. Cas. 660. Followed in an Australian appeal: *Wilfley Ore Concentrator Syndicate Ltd.* v. *Guthridge*, [1906] A.C. 548.

[7] *Clergue* v. *Murray*, [1903] A.C. 521. Followed for Australia in *Victorian Railways Commissioners* v. *Brown*, [1906] A.C. 38.

[8] *Taylor* v. *Attorney-General for Queensland*, [1918] W.N. 85.

are first drawn in the post-war cases. In *Whittaker* v. *Durban Corporation*[1] Lord Haldane, for the Board, said:

'The effect of the Confederation was to say that South Africa shall dispose of its own appeals. . . . No doubt the prerogative is not wholly swept away, but it is obviously intended [by s. 106] that it should be exercised in a very restricted sense. . . . In the South Africa Act of 1909 there is express power given to Parliament to limit the prerogative. That shows an intention that the matter should be looked at from a South African point of view.'

As the case raised 'essentially a local question', special leave was not granted. Even for Canada, the limits were drawn tighter, appeals being restricted to 'far-reaching questions of law or questions of dominant public importance'.[2] In *Hull* v. *McKenna*, in 1923,[3] Lord Haldane explained the reluctance of the Judicial Committee to hear South African appeals as arising from the fact that South Africa, unlike Canada, was a unitary Dominion.[4] The same reluctance, he said, would be shown in entertaining appeals from the Irish Free State, another unitary Dominion. He acknowledged that 'the desire of the people' of the Dominion was a factor to be considered in deciding what appeals should be admitted.[5]

These dicta are vague and somewhat conflicting, and must be taken rather as indicating the general policy of the board than as destroying its discretion for the future. Too much importance has been attached to Lord Haldane's dicta in *Hull* v. *McKenna*,[6] which were clearly extempore and not intended to establish fixed principles of law. If they and similar dicta are taken as law, there is ground for the Irish complaint[7] that special leave should not have been given in *Lynam* v. *Butler (No. 1)*[8] and in *Moore* v. *Attorney-General of the Irish Free State*,[9] but not for the similar complaints that were made against the granting of special leave in the other Irish cases of *Wigg and Cochrane* v. *Attorney-General of the Irish Free State*[10] and *Performing Right*

---

[1] (1920) 90 L.J. (P.C.) 119; 36 T.L.R. 784.

[2] *Albright* v. *Hydro-Electric Power Company of Ontario*, [1923] A.C. 167.

[3] 67 Sol. J. 801; [1926] I.R. 402.

[4] This was a better explanation than that which he had given in *Whittaker* v. *Durban Corporation*, for the intention to restrict appeals is even more clearly shown in the Australian Constitution than in the South Africa Act. Yet Australia is treated in this matter like Canada, not like South Africa.

[5] [1926] I.R. 402, 405. This criterion, strictly applied, would have prevented the hearing of any appeals from the Irish Free State.   [6] Loc. cit.

[7] Made notably by Mr. Hector Hughes in *Judicial Autonomy in the British Commonwealth of Nations*, pp. 80 sqq.

[8] [1925] 2 I.R. 231.   [9] [1935] A.C. 484; [1934] 2 I.R. 472.

[10] [1927] A.C. 74; [1927] I.R. 285.

Society v. *Bray*[1] and in the South African case of *Pearl Assurance Co.* v. *Union Government.*[2]

Appeals in criminal cases are only entertained by the Judicial Committee where 'justice itself in its very foundations has been subverted'.[3]

Examination of the number of cases actually decided by the Judicial Committee in recent years shows that there is a considerable annual flow of appeals from Canada, and (considering the relative populations) a proportionate number from New Zealand, whose greater distance is compensated by the fact that appeals lie from its Supreme Court as of right. Australia, owing to its distance and to the restrictions on constitutional appeals, sends rather less than half as many in proportion. South African cases are very rare. There is a spate of appeals from India, which even the establishment of the new Federal Court may not suffice to check.[4]

There were times in the latter half of the nineteenth century when the reputation of the Judicial Committee was not high. The personnel of the Board was often senile and undistinguished; and it was said that the single-judgment rule had been providentially devised to enable all except the member who was going to write the judgment to sleep during the hearing.[5] In the twentieth century ground for these criticisms gradually disappeared, but until quite recently the complaint could still be heard that the law lords treated their duties on the Board as a holiday from their duties in the House, and that boards of three were set up to hear appeals from distinguished full benches of four, five, or six in the Dominions. But at the present time it is probably true to say that the Judicial Committee, which is formally the equal of the House of Lords, enjoys very nearly the same prestige in the opinion of the profession.[6] The single-judgment rule[7] tends to make a Privy Council decision more impersonal and a little cruder,[8] but considerably simpler and therefore more intel-

---

[1] [1930] A.C. 377; [1930] I.R. 509.   [2] [1934] A.C. 571.

[3] Lord Shaw of Dunfermline in *Arnold* v. *King-Emperor*, [1914] A.C. 644, 650. See also *R.* v. *Bertrand* (1867) L.R. 1 P.C. 520, 529 sqq. and two recent cases, *Attygalle* v. *R.*, [1936] A.C. 338 and *Renouf* v. *Attorney-General for Jersey*, [1936] A.C. 445.

[4] For statistics of the origin of appeals, see Note II, below, p. 575.

[5] These faults did not go unnoticed in the Dominions. Cf., e.g., Senator Sir R. W. Scott in *Canadian Senate Debates*, 4th April 1894, p. 37.

[6] Its decisions, of course, are not imperatively binding on English and Scottish courts, nor are those of English and Scottish courts, including the House of Lords, on it.

[7] See above, p. 546.

[8] e.g. *King* v. *Victoria Insurance Company*, [1896] A.C. 250, and *Victorian Railway Commissioners* v. *Coultas* (1888) 3 App. Cas. 222.

ligible than the handful of three to five judgments which constitutes a decision of the House of Lords. Unlike the House, the Judicial Committee does not regard itself as imperatively bound by its own past decisions.[1] These peculiarities save it from becoming enmeshed in precedent's most complex nets,[2] and add to the authority of its decisions in appeals from primitive peoples on broad questions of justice and right. But the single-judgment rule makes its decisions on fine points in developed legal systems less copious, and therefore sometimes less instructive than those of the House of Lords.

It might be expected that the Judicial Committee would show less competence in alien laws than it does in the common law. But its reputation in Roman-Dutch law is high, both among scholars in that doctrine[3] and among those members of the profession who practise in it.[4] Between the private law of South Africa and the private law of England there is not, despite appearances, so great a gulf as that which divides public law under a rigid constitution from public law under full parliamentary sovereignty. Consideration of the competence of the Judicial Committee in this other exotic sphere will be postponed to a later stage of the argument.[5]

The Privy Council is often criticized for its expense. Its costs, by English standards, are not excessive. But litigation is notoriously expensive in England, more expensive than in any of the countries from which appeals to the Privy Council come.[6] Leave to appeal or defend *in forma pauperis* may be given by the Board, but only to parties who show that they are not worth £25 in the world, except their wearing apparel.[7] There is, of course, a large class of persons not paupers by this definition who cannot possibly face the costs of an appeal. The existence of the Privy Council appeal thus considerably increases the advantage of the rich over the poor litigant. Comparatively little hardship of this kind occurs, however, in constitutional cases. The protagonists in constitutional questions are usually public

---

[1] e.g. *Russell* v. *R.* (1882) 7 App. Cas. 829, and *Toronto Electric Commissioners* v. *Snider*, [1925] A.C. 396.

[2] An impasse such as that which arose in the reluctant attempt of the House of Lords in *Great Western Railway* v. *Mostyn*, [1928] A.C. 57, to discover a ratio decidendi in the conflicting judgments of *River Wear Commissioners* v. *Adamson* (1877) 2 App. Cas. 743, could not occur in the Privy Council.

[3] e.g. R. W. Lee in 51 *L.Q.R.* 274, 52 *S. Afr. Law Journ.* 318.

[4] But the Judicial Committee is criticized for applying to the Quebec Civil Code the rigid English canons of statutory interpretation, which are contrary to the traditions of French civil law: Mr. Justice Mignault in 1 *University of Toronto Law Journ.* 104.

[5] See below, pp. 560–3, 565–71.   [6] Except perhaps Canada.

[7] Such leave entitles the pauper to have solicitor and counsel assigned to him, and relieves him from all fees payable to the Privy Council office, but not from the expenses of preparing and printing the record.

bodies or other parties of substance, and where the nominal parties are men of straw, they are usually supported by adequately wealthy interests. In any event, it is so much in the public interest that constitutional decisions should be of the highest available quality that, if the Privy Council appeal contributes to that end, a good case can be made out for its continuance despite some hardship to individual litigants—if, indeed, such hardship is unavoidable. These considerations do not apply with equal force to appeals in private law.[1]

Because its jurisdiction cuts across the division of the Empire into those six autonomous units which are called the members of the Commonwealth, the Privy Council is necessarily praised and criticized not only by the standards which are applied to domestic courts, but in the light of the different views that are held of what the nature of the Commonwealth is, and of what it ought to be. It is not our present purpose to choose between imperialism, nationalism, and provincialism, but to discover how far the Privy Council jurisdiction can properly be said to further or to frustrate the cause of each.

Those whose chief concern is the unity of the Empire usually approve of the Privy Council jurisdiction. Three senses may be distinguished, in decreasing order of concreteness, in which the Privy Council is thought to promote Empire unity: it is regarded as a safeguard of unity, as a symbol of unity, and as an influence for solidarity of law.

The value of the Privy Council as a direct constitutional safeguard of imperial unity has been consistently overestimated in the United Kingdom since the earliest times. Vaughan, C.J., in 1674 assigned the following lucid reasons why English courts should supervise the courts of the colonies:[2]

> 'The reasons are, First for that without such writ, the Law appointed or permitted to such inferiour Dominion, might be insensibly changed within it self, without the assent of the Dominion Superiour. Secondly, Judgments might be then given to the disadvantage or lessening of the Superiority, which cannot be reasonable; or to make the Superiority to be only of the King, and not of the Crown of England (as King James once would have it in the case of Ireland, *ex relatione J. Selden mihi*, whom King James consulted in this Question).'

[1] Professor R. W. Lee informs the writer that the Privy Council has occasionally given special leave to appeal from the Supreme Court of Canada, where one of the parties was a wealthy corporation, only on the terms that the appellant pay the costs of both sides *in any event*.

[2] Vaugh. 395, 402.

This dictum referred to the jurisdiction of the common law courts of England to grant prerogative writs and writs of error running to the colonies, and as a statement of law it was already out of date when spoken, for this theoretical jurisdiction never really worked in relation to the 'plantations'.[1] As an expression of the reasons why imperialists support the Privy Council jurisdiction, it might have been uttered yesterday. But how effective has the Privy Council been to prevent these mischiefs ? There could be no neater description of the developments in the Irish Free State and South Africa, discussed in the previous section, than that 'the Law appointed or permitted to the inferiour Dominion' has been 'insensibly changed within it self, without the assent of the Dominion Superiour'. What, again, are the decisions of the Board itself in *Moore* v. *Attorney-General of the Irish Free State*[2] and *British Coal Corporation* v. *R.*[3] but 'Judgments . . . given to the disadvantage or lessening of the Superiority'? And could there be clearer examples than the Irish Free State Constitution and the Status of the Union Act of measures 'to make the Superiority to be only of the King, and not of the Crown of England'? For the most part, it is true, the emancipation of the Dominions has been carried out by processes with which no court could interfere: by unequivocal legislation, which courts have to accept, and by the development of conventions, of which they can take only tardy notice, if indeed they can notice them at all. But where the law has been doubtful, the Board has usually preferred the view according the largest measure of autonomy, and it is arguable that in the two recent cases cited it even strained the law in favour of the plenitude of Dominion power.[4]

A symbol, like a metaphor, cannot be called true or untrue, but is judged by its felicity. And a symbol of unity, however felicitous it may be in the abstract, fails if it has not a universal appeal to those whom it purports to unite. The Privy Council jurisdiction is in the abstract a very felicitous symbol of imperial unity. The fiction that the appellant to the Judicial Committee is bringing his grievance to the very foot of the Throne has a particular charm not only for primitive peoples, but for that majority of the inhabitants of the Empire which has not read the iconoclastic judgment of the Board in *British Coal Corporation* v. *The King*.[5] But in the first place, the

[1] See above, p. 519.   [2] [1935] A.C. 484.   [3] [1935] A.C. 500.
[4] W. I. Jennings in 52 *L.Q.R.* 173; V. C. MacDonald in 13 *Can. Bar Rev.* 625; Mr. Justice Dixon in 10 *Aust. Law Journ., Supp.* 96.
[5] [1935] A.C. 500. In which several of the traditional doctrines concerning the Board were declared to be obsolete fictions even in the eyes of the law. Below, pp. 613-14.

E

suggestion of centralized power[1] was more appropriate to the old-style unity, which was imperialistic in the strict sense, than to the new unity-in-equality of the Commonwealth. Further, as we have seen, the principle of equality is not at all adequately represented in the composition of the Board. The Lord Chief Justice of England[2] and the Board in *British Coal Corporation* v. *R.*,[3] do it is true, by an effort of abstraction, see in the Judicial Committee not what is in effect a United Kingdom tribunal, but a true Commonwealth court. The average Dominion citizen, however, does not.[4] To Dominion nationalists, including many who are well disposed to imperial unity, the symbolism of the Privy Council jurisdiction seems definitely infelicitous.[5] The case for the Privy Council appeal as a symbol of unity in the Commonwealth accordingly fails. Its symbolic value for the dependent empire of the United Kingdom is, however, great.[6]

The Privy Council has a very real and important influence in maintaining uniformity in law and in standards of justice. But these benefits, though often stressed by imperialists, stand really upon their own feet, and could consistently be, although they seldom are, equally appreciated by those to whom imperial unity as a general objective makes no appeal. They will accordingly not be considered under the present head.

Over against imperialism—though not by any means necessarily in conflict with it—stands Dominion nationalism, certainly the most real and effective political force in British Commonwealth relations at the present time. The old formal nationalist argument against the

---

[1] Cf. above, p. 556 n.

[2] Lord Hewart, L.C.J., speaking extra-judicially at Johannesburg on 26 August 1936, said, 'No fallacy could be more complete or gratuitous than that which assumes or implies that appeal to the Privy Council is an appeal to England from some other part of the British Commonwealth of Nations.' Mentioning the fact that Dominion judges sit on the Board, he continues, 'The learning, experience and wisdom of the whole are brought to bear in the interests of any particular part' (*The Times*, 27 August 1936). If for 'England' we read 'English, Scottish, and Anglo-Indian judges' the 'fallacy' becomes substantially true. See Note III, below, p. 575.

[3] [1935] A.C. 500.

[4] For a summary by a French Canadian nationalist of expressions of hostility to the appeal, see Ollivier, *Le Canada, pays souverain ?*' ch. xvii, passim.

[5] For example, the juristic sub-committee of the unofficial Toronto Conference of 1933 (at which the Irish Free State was not represented), which went much farther than the Imperial Conference of 1930 in its desire to see established a permanent tribunal for inter-imperial disputes, rules out the Privy Council at the very beginning of its deliberations, for the reason stated in the text. See Toynbee, *British Commonwealth Relations*, pp. 85 sqq., 196 sqq.

[6] Note that India is, by comparison, well represented on the board which hears Indian appeals. Indeed, the board is often no less Indian in its composition than the court from which the appeal is brought. See above, loc. cit.

Privy Council jurisdiction—namely, that the mere existence of an uncontrollable external appellate tribunal is a limitation of Dominion autonomy—is, for what it is worth, unanswerable. The Board itself, in *British Coal Corporation* v. *R.*,[1] has admitted as much:

> 'Among the powers which go to constitute self-government there are necessarily included powers to constitute the Law Courts and to regulate their procedure. . . . A most essential part of the administration of justice consists of the system of appeals. . . . Such appeals seem to be essentially matters of Canadian concern, and the regulation and control of such appeals would thus seem to be a prime element in Canadian sovereignty as appertaining to matters of justice.'

As we have seen,[2] the extent to which such a theoretical limitation of self-government is also a practical one depends on the degree in which the prevalent ideal of law and justice departs from pure objectivity, and that in turn depends upon the temperament of the people. But the limitation has now ceased even in a formal sense to be an external limitation, since all the Dominions may now abolish the Privy Council appeal at least as easily as they can alter their constitutions in other respects.[3]

There remains, however, the substantial question, how far it is wise for a Dominion to let appeals from its courts to the Privy Council continue. Nationalism is, of course, only one factor, but so far as nationalism is concerned, the issue becomes: will the full and free development of the nation be hindered by the continuance of appeals? As we have already seen, a Dominion which is interested in the formal aspect of national independence may wish to establish its right of secession in strict law.[4] To establish this it will need to put itself outside the formal unity of Empire law; and this delicate process might be embarrassed by the Privy Council.[5] We have further seen that, apart from the matter of formal unity, the Judicial Committee is neither directly able to restrict the emancipation of the Dominions to any considerable extent, nor, to the extent that it is able, does it seem disposed to do so.[6] But the really important influence of the Privy Council is a more subtle one, lying outside the sphere of the law of the imperial constitution. In its jurisdiction over the domestic constitutional law and the private law of the Dominions, will the Judicial Committee take an 'anti-national' or an insufficiently 'national' line? This is the central question, by the answer to which the attitude of every Dominion to the Privy Council will,

[1] [1935] A.C. 500, 520–1.
[2] See above, pp. 541–3.
[3] See above, pp. 550–2.
[4] See above, pp. 527–8.
[5] See above, p. 545.
[6] See above, p. 557.

rightly or wrongly, in the long run be chiefly determined. Like most other questions concerning the Privy Council, it is governed by different considerations in the spheres of constitutional interpretation and of private law.

The relevance of nationalism to private law is at the present time universally exaggerated. Countries which have identical social and commercial systems require and achieve legal systems which are in fact closely similar, however nomenclature and adjective details may differ. Even on the continent of Europe, where general national traditions are strong and legal origins fairly diverse, the elements of *jurisprudence* that are genuinely national in their inspiration are very small, and amount in the last analysis to little more than local colour. The insistence that German law and German judgments should smack of 'blood and soil' make them not more German, but only worse judgments and worse law. Still less does a system like the Common Law, whose methodology is more peculiar and more resistant than that of the Civil Law systems of Europe, suffer upon transplantation sufficient modification of its spirit for it to be possible to speak of a rule of law as having a specifically Australian, or Canadian, or even American quality.

Nationalism is, however, highly relevant to public law, especially to the law of federal or other rigid systems. Dominion public law differs from the public law of the United Kingdom in omitting many ornamental institutions, and, in the case of the federal Dominions, adding a vast superstructure to support the federal system. In that part of the law which is common to both, namely, the rules determining the general character of legislature, executive, and judiciary and the general principles of administrative law, there is very little variation from the British model.[1] Even the Irish Free State, with the best will in the world to depart from British traditions wherever possible, has in fact followed British law and tradition closely for want of an available alternative.[2] But the superadded *corpus* of funda-

[1] Some departments of English public law which have been taken over by the Dominions have, however, reached a higher stage of development there. Note, for instance, the number of Australian decisions on the writ of prohibition. The law relating to injunctions in political cases needs, and will probably receive, clarification at the hands of Dominion courts. See Evatt, *The King and his Dominion Governors*, pp. 289, 290.

[2] e.g. *Leen* v. *President of the Executive Council*, [1926] I.R. 456 (the Free State has the same immunity from discovery as the Crown in England), *Carolan* v. *Minister of Defence*, [1927] I.R. 62 (the common law rule that superior servants of the Crown are not liable for the torts of inferior servants applies in the Free State), *Attorney-General* v. *O'Kelly*, [1928] I.R. 308 (Superior courts in the Free State have power to

mental constitutional law in the federal Dominions, is not only for the most part without parallel in British law so far as its actual rules are concerned, but differs in kind, in that there is no available legislature which can conveniently change those rules if, as interpreted by the courts, they are found to be unworkable. If interpretation of a British domestic statute by an English court renders the statute unworkable or frustrates the intention of its framers, it is possible, with a little trouble, to put an amendment through Parliament which will rectify the defect. The courts' traditional attitude of slight hostility to statute law, though awkward for administrators, is occasionally a safeguard of civil liberties, and always a useful discipline for draftsmen. The delay in carrying out the intention of the legislature is only temporary. But if the courts treat a rigid constitution in the same way—if they 'construe it as they would construe a Dog Act'—no such remedy is available. In Canada and Australia the difficulty of the process of constitutional amendment is such that in practice only non-contentious amendments can succeed. The courts are accordingly compelled in fact to adopt comparatively liberal rules of construction, whether or not they acknowledge them openly. The working of the constitution cannot be lightly wrecked because its framers occasionally expressed themselves unclearly, and did not foresee future circumstances. The difficulty of altering constitutional provisions means that, if they are literally construed, the constitution runs the risk of becoming out of harmony with contemporary conditions. In fact, the tendency of political opinion and economic forces in the two federal Dominions has been towards centralization. 'Progressive' interpretation of their constitutions will accordingly have a centralizing tendency. This tendency is readily identified, in public and professional opinion, with nationalism. In another age, nationalism and modernity may not coincide; for the moment, they do.

To the extent, then, that the Privy Council makes its interpretation of rigid constitutions march with the times, it will win the approval of nationalists. It must not be thought that such a demand is necessarily a demand for an illicit adulteration of law with politics. Statutes cannot be interpreted by their own light alone, and least of all can national constitutions. 'Where the text is explicit, the text is conclusive'—agreed. But where the text is inexplicit, one must

commit for contempt, whether or not that power is derived from the fiction of the presence of the King in Court), *State* (*Ryan*) v. *Lennon*, [1935] I.R. 170 (in the Free State Constitution, the principle of parliamentary sovereignty is more fundamental than the principle of fundamental rights).

look outside it. *Heydon's Case*[1] itself, the leading case of all our law of statutory interpretation, bids the court ascertain the mischief which the statute was designed to remedy, and adopt that construction of its terms which will best suppress the mischief and advance the remedy. The mischiefs against which the British North America Act, 1867, and the Commonwealth of Australia Constitution Act, 1900, were passed were the lack of political organisms corresponding to the geographical unities of the Canadian and Australian colonies. The remedy chosen in each case was to set up a national government for the common purposes. To assert, therefore, that the effective operation of the national system of government as a whole should be a postulate of constitutional construction is no violation even of the English tradition of statutory interpretation.

The problem for the nationalist is not to estimate the absolute degree in which the Judicial Committee complies with this requirement, but to compare it in this respect with the only available alternative courts of final appeal, namely the highest courts of the Dominions. There is no need to make this comparison in the abstract, for in the treatment of Canadian appeals by the Judicial Committee and of Australian appeals by the High Court of Australia we have an experience which is almost equivalent to a 'controlled' laboratory experiment. The ensuing account of how each tribunal has served its Dominion will also illustrate the merits of each tribunal from other points of view than that of nationalism.

Each had to find its bearings in strange seas, and each (except the High Court in its earliest years) chose to regard those seas as uncharted, though the rich experience of the United States was at hand.[2] It is therefore not surprising that neither has steered a course which can be described as straight. It is still too early to say whether their vagaries will ever be able to be regarded retrospectively as adroit tacking towards a definite goal, or whether they will appear to have been drifting at the mercy of wind and waves. Each tribunal has, alike for its inconsistencies and for its consistencies, been subjected to intense criticism from within and without the legal profession. Owing to the wide extent and highly litigious character of Australian industrial law, the High Court has come more often

[1] (1584) 3 Co. Rep. 7a, at 7b.

[2] The Privy Council, with considerable justification, never regarded United States authorities as applying at all closely to the Canadian constitution, a document of a very different type. On the other hand, the provisions of the Australian Constitution relating to the federal system as such follow the American constitution closely. The High Court followed American precedents in its early years, but abandoned them—in the opinion of the writer, without sufficient justification—in 1921.

into the arena of controversy. Bùt so far as popular criticism at least is concerned, these attacks have usually spent their main force on the Arbitration Court, which has thus acted as a shock-absorber. In fact the Judicial Committee is probably more criticized, though, being remote from the scene and a body of shifting composition, it is less sensible of the fact. Neither court has ever incurred a tenth of the odium which is being heaped upon the Supreme Court of the United States at the present time.

The original bench of the High Court of Australia,[1] maturely wise without excess of cleverness, treated the constitution as a federal compact and saved as far as possible the integrity of both States and Commonwealth by applying the American doctrine of the immunity of federal and state instrumentalities, a sort of rule of mutual tolerance.[2] A brilliant minority, appointed to the bench in 1906, broke British judicial tradition by persisting in consistent dissent.[3] They repeatedly refused to recognize previous majority decisions *in pari materia* as binding in subsequent cases, and elaborated an heretical doctrine in exhaustive dissenting judgments.[4] As the older judges left the bench, and new appointments were made, this solid minority became the majority. The revolutionary *Engineers' Case*[5] in 1921 marks the point at which their heterodoxy became the new orthodoxy. The reasoning of this decision is open to all sorts of criticism. The case was decided on high constitutional ground, when a much simpler argument would have sufficed.[6] It cut off Australian constitutional law from American precedents, a copious source of thoroughly relevant learning, in favour of the crabbed English rules of statutory interpretation, which are one of the sorriest features of English law, and are, as we have seen, particularly unsuited to the interpretation of a rigid constitution. The majority judgment was, further, self-contradictory in two ways. It declared that the Constitution was

[1] Sir Samuel Griffith, Sir Edmund Barton, and Mr. Justice R. E. O'Connor.

[2] *D'Emden* v. *Pedder* (1904) 1 C.L.R. 91; *Deakin* v. *Webb* (1904) 1 C.L.R. 595; *Railway Servants' Case* (1906) 4 C.L.R. 488.

[3] Sir Isaac Isaacs and the late Mr. Justice H. B. Higgins.

[4] Such persistence in dissent is, however, usual in the Supreme Court of the United States.

[5] *Amalgamated Society of Engineers* v. *Adelaide S.S. Co.*, 28 C.L.R. 129. The actual decision was that the wages and conditions of labour laid down in an award of the Commonwealth Court of Conciliation and Arbitration set up by the Commonwealth Parliament under s. 51, pl. xxxv, of the Constitution bound the state of Western Australia as an employer in respect of its State saw-mills.

[6] It could have been decided on the ground that running saw-mills was a non-governmental activity involving no element of sovereignty, in respect of which the state stood in the same position as any other employer.

to be interpreted by its words alone; yet the court. in reaching that very proposition, took notice of responsible government, a matter far more extrinsic to strict law, and far less admissible by the English rules of statutory construction themselves, than the close verbal correspondence with the United States Constitution upon which the early High Court had relied[1] to bring American authorities in point. And this very judgment which abandoned American precedents would not have been possible if the majority had not followed the loose American rather than the strict English view of the binding authority of precedent.[2] The fundamental criticism of the decision is that its real ground is nowhere stated in the majority judgment. This real ground was the view held by the majority that the Constitution had been intended to create a nation, and that it had succeeded; that in the Great War the nation had in fact advanced in status while the states stood still, and (as was a patent fact) that the peace had not brought a relapse into the *status quo ante bellum*; that a merely contractual view of the Constitution was therefore out of date, and its persistence in the law was stultifying the Commonwealth industrial power, which they believed to be a real and vital power; and finally, that the words of the Constitution permitted the view of the federal relationship which the times demanded. A judgment on these lines would have made the *Engineers' Case* frankly a quasi-political decision, based on a far-sighted view of ultimate constitutional policy, of the type with which the Supreme Court of the United States in its greatest periods has made us familiar. It would have been no more political than several of Sir Isaac Isaac's most notable judgments, and, so far as judicial recognition of a constitutional *fait accompli* is concerned, there is good American precedent in *Texas* v. *White*.[3] The Judicial Committee has since shown itself almost as radical in *British Coal Corporation* v. *R*.[4] The majority judgment, however, still stands as it was given. There having been no more accessions of crusading judges, the High Court has returned to more or less orthodox principles of *stare decisis*,[5] and as a consequence the expressed *ratio decidendi* of that judgment remains as the leading authority in the law of the federal relationship. The actual power of the Commonwealth was notably advanced by *New South Wales* v. *Commonwealth*

---

[1] *D'Emden* v. *Pedder* (1904) 1 C.L.R. 91.   [2] See above, p. 563, n. 4.
[3] (1868) 7 Wall. 700.   [4] [1935] A.C. 500.
[5] For example, the court which threw over all existing precedents to decide the *Engineers' Case* would not have felt bound, as did the court in *James* v. *Commonwealth*, 52 C.L.R. 570, to follow its own decisions despite its disagreement with them, and ask the Privy Council to deliver it from chains of its own forging.

(*No.* 1),[1] a decision in the political crisis of 1932 upon the new section 105A of the Constitution which opens up the possibility that financial agreements under that section might be construed to authorize the Commonwealth to override almost any right of the States incidentally to the execution of the agreements. The recent *Aviation Case*,[2] which decides that the Commonwealth may under its power to legislate for external affairs legislate in execution of international conventions in excess of the domestic powers otherwise granted to it, marks yet another substantial access of power to the Commonwealth. In its construction of particular heads of Commonwealth legislative power, notably of the industrial arbitration power, the High Court has taken a generous line.[3] But the general principle that residuary power is in the States remains uninfringed, and applies even to matters which are utterly unsuited for local control, if they cannot be brought under any explicit head of Commonwealth power.[4]

On another major topic of the Constitution, namely, the provision in section 92 that 'trade, commerce, and intercourse between the States shall be absolutely free', the High Court in its middle period gave a number of mutually inconsistent decisions[5] which embarrassed it when it returned to the orthodox calculus of precedent. In *James* v. *Commonwealth*[6] it felt itself bound by its past decisions to give a decision which it thought wrong in principle, and at the same time expressed a hope that the Privy Council (whose aid in constitutional cases it had not been in the habit of welcoming)[7] would reverse it on appeal[8].

It is not fair to take the judgments of the Privy Council in Australian constitutional appeals as samples of its quality as an interpreter of fundamental law. The situation by which the decision of the central questions of the Constitution are assigned to a court which is in other respects of inferior rank, the superior court being only let in on peripheral issues, is unfortunate in every way. In

---

[1] 46 C.L.R. 155.

[2] *R.* v. *Burgess, ex p. Henry* (1936) 10 Aust. Law Journ. 335.

[3] In establishing that the nature of the power authorized by the Constitution to be conferred upon the Commonwealth Court of Conciliation and Arbitration is essentially legislative and not judicial, the High Court has made a notable advance on its early dicta, for which advance Sir Isaac Isaacs is chiefly to be thanked.

[4] *R.* v. *Burgess, ex p. Henry*, cited above.

[5] The *Wheat Case* (1915) 20 C.L.R. 54; *Foggitt Jones and Co.* v. *New South Wales* (1916) 21 C.L.R. 357; *Duncan* v. *Queensland* (1916) 22 C.L.R. 556, and *McArthur's Case* (1920) 28 C.L.R. 530 are some of them.

[6] (1935) 52 C.L.R. 570.

[7] *Flint* v. *Webb* (1907) 4 C.L.R. 1178.

[8] The Privy Council did: *James* v. *Commonwealth*, [1936] A.C. 578.

such circumstances it was inevitable that the judgments of the Privy Council should be desultory and lacking in profundity, as they have indeed been. This is in itself no proof that, had the Judicial Committee been entrusted with a general jurisdiction over the Australian Constitution, it would not have done much better. There is the further consolation that the quality of the decisions has steadily improved. The first was the worst. *Webb* v. *Outtrim*[1] contained one major blunder,[2] and showed complete incomprehension both of the reasoning which led the High Court to apply American authority to the Australian Constitution and of American constitutional doctrine itself, which is on any view a necessary background to the study of any rigid constitution under the common law. The latter errors were adequately exposed by the High Court in *Baxter* v. *Federal Commissioner of Taxation*,[3] and the decision was politely ignored thereafter.[4] Behind the greater sophistication of the *Sugar Case*[5] of 1915 there are concealed some fundamental errors springing from narrowness of outlook.[6] The decision of the Board in *Shell Co.* v. *Federal Commissioner of Taxation*[7] was neither better nor worse than that of the High Court[8] which it affirmed: the judgments in both courts were unanalytical and barren,[9] though right in the result. *Attorney-General for New South Wales* v. *Trethowan*[10] was rightly decided, but the opinion showed such excessive timidity that it hardly amounts to a statement of reasons for judgment at all.[11] *James* v. *Cowan*,[12] a sound decision on the freedom of interstate trade clause, failed to bring that illumination from above which alone

---

[1] [1907] A.C. 81.

[2] The view, expressed at p. 88, that the royal assent to a statute ousts judicial review. Lord Halsbury, L.C., during the argument said, in reply to counsel's contention that a law was *ultra vires*: 'That is a novelty to me. I thought an Act of Parliament was an Act of Parliament and you cannot go beyond it. . . . I do not know what an unconstitutional act means.' Quoted in Ollivier, *Le Canada, pays souverain ?*, p. 223.

[3] (1908) 4 C.L.R. 1087.

[4] The majority judgment in the *Engineers' Case*, 28 C.L.R. 129, although it upset the rule in *Baxter's Case*, adopted another ground, despite the courteous mention of *Webb* v. *Outtrim* at p. 150. It is regrettable that the Supreme Court of Canada should have based its decision in *Abbott* v. *City of St. John* (1908) 40 S.C.R. 597 on *Webb* v. *Outtrim*. See also *Attorney-General for Manitoba* v. *Worthington* (1934) 42 Manitoba Reports 540.

[5] *Attorney-General for the Commonwealth* v. *Colonial Sugar Refining Co.*, [1914] A.C. 237.

[6] See 9 *Aust. Law Journ.* 213, 248, and for a Canadian criticism of some dicta, Kennedy; *Essays in Constitutional Law*, pp. 36 sqq.

[7] [1931] A.C. 275.   [8] (1926) 38 C.L.R. 153.

[9] Cf. J. Finkelman, 1 *University of Toronto Law Journal*, pp. 339–40.

[10] [1932] A.C. 526. A case on a State constitution.

[11] Cf. above, p. 523.   [12] [1932] A.C. 542.

could have led the High Court out of its perplexities. The latest decision, *James* v. *Commonwealth*,[1] on another aspect of the same clause, is the best Australian constitutional decision of the Privy Council to date: it is nevertheless not a great decision.

The Judicial Committee has occasionally been criticized by Australian lawyers for greediness of jurisdiction. Its entertaining an appeal on an *inter se* question direct from a state court[2] was thought to be against the spirit of the Constitution at least, and the leak was stopped by an ingenious legislative device.[3] In the *Sugar Case*,[4] which is the only appeal which has gone to the Judicial Committee by certificate of the High Court under section 74 of the Constitution, the Judicial Committee went beyond its terms of reference in the High Court's certificate.[5] The decision that the question in *James* v. *Cowan*[6] was not an *inter se* question, and was therefore entertainable by the Judicial Committee, proceeded on narrow grounds, and was open to criticism in the then state of the law.

Objective comparison of the Supreme Court of Canada with the Judicial Committee and the High Court of Australia in respect of policy is almost impossible for the student, since the general appeal to the Privy Council has deprived the Supreme Court of the opportunity to form its own *jurisprudence*. Of the comparative merits of the Supreme Court and the Privy Council as tribunals there is deep division of professional opinion. Probably a majority would agree that for sheer competence in law the Judicial Committee is definitely superior; though some would say that the English tradition of competent lawyership, when applied without adjustment to the construction of constitutions, produces nothing more than dexterous but purblind manipulation of imperfectly analysed and over-literal concepts. These critics would go on to assert that the Supreme Court, if left to itself in constitutional matters, would develop a liberal tradition in constitutional interpretation whose value would outweigh any comparative deficiency it may have shown in the field of ordinary law.

The history of Privy Council interpretation of the Canadian consti-

[1] [1936] A.C. 578. [2] *Webb* v. *Outtrim*, above.

[3] See above, p. 549, n. 1.

[4] *Attorney-General for the Commonwealth* v. *Colonial Sugar Refining Co.*, [1914] A.C. 237, 15 C.L.R. 182.

[5] The certificate is printed in 15 C.L.R. at p. 234. The criticism is suggested by J. G. Latham, *Australia and the British Commonwealth*, p. 115. But *quaere*, whether the High Court should have framed the certificate in such narrow terms. That, however, is a separate question.

[6] [1932] A.C. 542, 560.

tution falls into three periods, of which the third is just beginning. In 1935, Dean V. C. MacDonald was able to write as follows:[1]

'Up to the year 1925 the course of decision was marked by a definite increase of provincial jurisdiction, with a corresponding curtailment of Dominion jurisdiction; subsequent to that date the trend has been in the direction of expanding the jurisdiction of the Dominion with a corresponding contraction of provincial jurisdiction. The trend to 1925 was marked by three main processes:

(a) the declension of the general residuary power of the Dominion to the status of a reserve power to be used only in case of war, famine, pestilence, or other national emergency;

(b) the devitalization of the "trade and commerce" power to a point where its exercise was confined to supplementary Dominion powers elsewhere conferred;

(c) the enlargement of the provincial power over "property and civil rights" to the extent that "the real residuary power of legislation in normal times was held to be contained in the words 'property and civil rights'[2]."[3]

'The ebb-tide of Dominion power having reached its lowest mark with the *Snider Case* of 1925, that power has been borne along on a flowing tide of returning vitality which, if sustained, may yet give Canada the constitution which it was intended to have.... This pro-Dominion trend has manifested itself in judgments of the Privy Council which (a) enlarge the scope of the Dominion's residuary power, (b) affirm the Dominion's capacity to implement international engagements, (c) give great sweep to its "criminal law" power, and (d) *per dicta*, indicate (though without defining) that the "trade and commerce" power is not merely auxiliary but substantive.[4]

'Up until ten years ago the Privy Council approached the [British North America] Act as a statute to be treated "by the same methods of construction and exposition which they (courts of law) apply to other statutes".[5] Excluding extraneous evidence as to its purpose and meaning, they were compelled to seek for them in the text alone, aided only by the flickering illumination afforded by rules of textual construction evolved with respect to ordinary statutes. This literalistic approach held sway for over fifty years.... In 1930 the Privy Council broke away from its traditional approach and, *mirabile dictu*, promulgated the doc-

[1] In 1 *University of Toronto Law Journal* 260, at pp. 276–8.
[2] H. A. Smith, *The Residue of Power in Canada*, 4 *Can. Bar Rev.* 432 sqq.
[3] e.g., *In re Board of Commerce Act*, [1922] 1 A.C. 191; *Toronto Electric Commissioners* v. *Snider*, [1925] A.C. 396.
[4] This tendency has manifested itself in a dictum in *Edwards* v. *Attorney-General for Canada*, [1930] A.C. 124, 136–7, and in the decisions of *Proprietary Articles Trade Association* v. *Attorney-General for Canada*, [1931] A.C. 310; the *Aeronautics Case*, [1932] A.C. 54; the *Radio Case*, [1932] A.C. 304; and *British Coal Corporation* v. *R.*, [1935] A.C. 500.
[5] *Bank of Toronto* v. *Lambe* (1887) 2 App. Cas. 575, 579.

trine that the Act is a constitution as well as a statute. "The British North America Act", said Lord Sankey, L.C., "planted in Canada *a living tree* capable of growth and expansion within its natural limits. . . . Their Lordships do not conceive it to be the duty of this Board—it is certainly not their desire—to cut down the provisions of the Act by a narrow and technical construction, but rather to give it a large and liberal interpretation".[1]

In January 1937, however, in its judgments in a group of appeals[2] concerning the validity of what has been called the 'New Deal' legislation of the former Conservative government in Canada, the 'flowing tide of returning vitality' began to ebb. Of the four progressive trends enumerated by Dean MacDonald, three received setbacks. The Dominion residuary power was cut down and the provincial power over 'property and civil rights' erected again into something like a general and superior residuary power.[3] It was decided that the fact that the Dominion is under a treaty obligation (otherwise than as part of the British Empire)[4] to legislate in a certain way does not authorize Dominion legislation implementing the treaty to invade the sphere of 'property and civil rights' thus widely construed.[5] Hopes that the trade and commerce power might be construed as a reality were dashed.[6] Whether the 'living tree' has merely been lopped, and will grow again, or whether it has been killed entirely it is impossible to tell. These decisions are a reversion to provincialism, but not an unequivocal reversion to literalism.[7] One general fact at least emerges: it cannot now be said that the judicial policy of the Privy Council is more stable than that of the High Court of Australia.[8] The range of the High Court's oscillations has

---

[1] *Edwards' Case*, [1930] A.C. 124, 136.

[2] Reported in *The Times*, 29 January 1937 and in [1937] W.N. 53–9. They will be reported in [1937] A.C.

[3] *in re Weekly Rest in Industrial Undertakings Act, &c.*, [1937] W.N. 53; *in re Employment and Social Insurance Act* [1937] W.N. 58; *in re Natural Products Marketing Act*, [1937] W.N. 57.

[4] Express power to implement British Empire treaties is given to the Dominion by s. 132 of the British North America Act.

[5] 'For the purposes of . . . the distribution of legislative powers between the Dominion and the Provinces, there is no such thing as treaty legislation as such. . . . As a treaty deals with a particular class of subjects, so will the legislative power of performing it be ascertained': *in re Weekly Rest in Industrial Undertakings Act*, [1937] [W.N.] 53.   [6] *In re Natural Products Marketing Act*, [1937] W.N. 57.

[7] It is worth noting that the Board justified its decision in the Labour Conventions case (*in re Weekly Rest Act*, [1937] W.N. 53) by reference to the inviolability of the 'separate jurisprudence' of the provinces, especially Quebec. This is a political consideration, inappropriate to a truly literalist decision.

[8] At the same time, its instability is less unedifying. It may be that a militant minority fights for its view within the Board, as Isaacs and Higgins, JJ., fought on the High Court bench; but the single judgment rule prevents the world from knowing.

been greater, but their period has hitherto been longer, and they are less recent.

In the decade preceding 1937, the Dominion nationalist was not able to urge against the Privy Council as a present complaint that it did not understand the full responsibilities of a court that is set rigidly in authority over the institutions of a nation. That complaint will now again be heard, and the case for it will be at least arguable. The abolition of constitutional appeals would not, however, necessarily provide a remedy, for Canadian courts have been brought up in the tradition of the Privy Council's first period, to which the bulk of authoritative cases on the British North America Act still belongs. They have, quite properly, not shown many signs of originality or restiveness. It may therefore be doubted whether their decisions, even if made unappealable, would satisfy the *desiderata* of the nationalist without an alteration in their personnel which might have an adverse effect on the mere quality, apart from the tendency, of their decisions.

Apart altogether from its judicial policy, there are reasons why, in certain circumstances, a Dominion nationalist can validly object to the Privy Council appeal. The carrying of domestic cases to an external tribunal is undoubtedly an infringement of the perfection of the formal sovereignty of his Dominion —a fact to which he may or may not attach importance. If he wishes to assert a local root for his system of law, he will be well advised to keep appeals within his borders. And only if a government controls judicial appointments can it resort, in crisis, to the *ultima ratio* of packing the Bench.[1]

The third political attitude to which the Privy Council jurisdiction is relevant is provincialism, that is to say, attachment to the rights of local units as against the federations of which they form part. In the present state of the world, for both political and economic reasons, true provincialism is not an advancing cause. The tendency is for devotion to the local unit either to become a unique loyalty, thereby rising to the status of nationalism, or to be swallowed up in the nationalism of the larger body. The true provincialist has no scruples about calling in the aid of imperial institutions against the common enemy, which is nationalism focused upon the federation. Probably the truest provincialisms in the British Commonwealth are those of the Australian States and of Natal. The status of Natal is

On the other hand, it is quite possible, in view of the inconstancy of the composition of the Board, that its contradictory decisions are all unanimously reached.

[1] As was done by President Lincoln in the Civil War, in order to upset a decision that the United States could not validly issue paper money. See *Hepburn* v. *Griswold* (1870) 8 Wall. 604 and the *Legal Tender Cases* (1871) 11 Wall. 682; 12 Wall. 528.

not guaranteed by fundamental law. No court, therefore, can protect it.[1] In Australia, those who hold the creed of 'States' rights' often favour the extension of the Privy Council appeal,[2] but there is little probability of this occurring.

Particularist sentiment in Quebec is a provincialism so strong that it verges upon nationalism. Quebec has felt in the past that an external court gives better than any Canadian court could the security which it most values—the security that there will always be a political organism corresponding to French-Canadian culture. In this they are right in principle, for in any federation there is a tendency for judges appointed to federal courts by central government to have a national rather than a local outlook; and in practice, apart from the short period between 1931 and 1937, they have been well served by the Judicial Committee. At the same time, the belief, common in Great Britain, that all French Canadians frequently refer with emotion to 'le droit sacré d'appel' is exaggerated. Among them the particularists à outrance are leaning at the moment to a common hostility to Dominion and Empire, while those who prefer to ally themselves with all-Canadian nationalism[3] can do so with less reserve than formerly, since the place of the French element in Canada's future is now in any event firmly assured.[4] The application of the Statute of Westminster to Canada, which necessarily added more to Dominion than to provincial power, was consented to by Quebec. It is therefore now quite possible that, if abolition or further limitation of the Privy Council jurisdiction for Canada is thought desirable on nationalist grounds, Quebec will not stand in the way.[5]

There remains the less obtrusive, but in solid fact by far the most important function of the Privy Council appeal—its function in maintaining the unity, and therefore the quality, of the private law of the common law countries of the Empire, and of that part of British public law which all the Empire shares. Few laymen realize that this function exists, and many lawyers underestimate its im-

[1] Nevertheless, Natal provincialists are attached to the Privy Council appeal.
[2] e.g. W. A. Holman, *The Australian Constitution* (Brisbane, 1928), p. 81; T. C. Brennan, *Interpreting the Constitution* (Sydney, 1935), ch. xxviii. Royal Commission on the Constitution, 1929, *Report*, p. 253.
[3] e.g. M. Maurice Ollivier, in *Le Canada, pays souverain?* (Montreal, 1935), ch. xvii.
[4] The proportion of French Canadians in the population of Canada (3,000,000 in 1936) is certainly not decreasing, and is probably increasing.
[5] It would be possible for Quebec to stand in the way not only if it turns out that provincial concurrence is necessary to the abolition of the appeal in civil matters (as to which see pp. 550–1 above) but by virtue of the strength of its representation in the Dominion parliament.

portance. It is known that the Judicial Committee occasionally corrects a rank miscarriage of justice which has occurred in some minor and remote jurisdiction. It is known, too, that in appeals from the more advanced of the dependencies and from the Dominions the daily work of the board is not so much the righting of plain injustice as the decision of refined points of law, and the significance of the jurisdiction for practising lawyers lies in the thin stream of decisions on such points, which enjoy high authority.

But it is wrong to regard the influence of an appellate court as merely corrective, or as operating only in the cases which actually come to it on appeal. The number of appeals it hears, and even the quality of its decisions, so long as it does not fall below a certain minimum level,[1] are more or less immaterial. The mere knowledge that there is a common appellate court above them whose decisions are not wholly capricious ensures that the courts below will adhere to certain standards of justice and of accuracy in law. In terms of the calculus of precedent, the potentiality of appeal to a common tribunal causes all courts below to accept its decisions as having binding authority, and each other's decisions as having stronger persuasive authority than decisions in an unconnected jurisdiction. The accident that the personnel of the Privy Council and the House of Lords are largely interchangeable[2] is in this respect most fortunate, for it creates an informal but effective link between the overseas jurisdictions which the Privy Council unites and the jurisdictions of the United Kingdom.[3]

A case-law system cannot flourish unless it has a continual stream of respectable reported decisions on all aspects of the law. In small isolated jurisdictions only the most litigated branches of the law remain living: the rest withers away. Because the appellate jurisdiction of the Privy Council renders the decisions of the courts of every (or nearly every) jurisdiction in the Empire available for the authoritative enlightenment of the other jurisdictions, it offers to the Dominions a disciplined wealth of precedent which enriches their local systems[4] to an extent otherwise impossible. In the United

[1] It is accordingly fallacious to imagine that advocacy of the Privy Council appeal in private law cases involves the imputation that the quality of Dominion justice is below that of the Privy Council. It may be even higher; the peculiar virtue of the Privy Council jurisdiction is not superlative quality, but its unifying effect.

[2] See Note IV, below, p. 576.

[3] The decisions of the Judicial Committee are not binding in Great Britain, nor are the decisions of the House of Lords overseas, but they are in each case of great persuasive authority. Decisions of British courts have high persuasive authority overseas, and the authority of Dominion judgments in England is growing.

[4] It is worth noting that no single overseas jurisdiction is comparable in size with

States there is an even greater—indeed, a quite embarrassing—wealth of case law. But owing to the lack of a single appellate court, the decisions of the courts of one State are under no obligation to agree with those of another, and each jurisdiction builds up for itself its own *jurisprudence*, differing in petty ways from that of the others. The Privy Council jurisdiction saves the Empire from this confusion.

Of course, this system imposes on the participant in it not only the merits of the common tradition of the common law, but its faults as well. Dominion courts, for example, are not free to develop for themselves a rational doctrine of statutory interpretation.[1] Defective rules of the common law can be, and regularly are, remedied by statutes. But those inarticulate defects which are inherent in the traditional approach of English courts to their work are not thus eradicable, and the existence of the Privy Council jurisdiction fastens them around the neck of every court in the Empire.[2]

But in general, in the opinion of the writer, so far as the private law of common law countries in the Empire is concerned, the advantages of the Privy Council appeal far outweigh its disadvantages, even when the hardship caused by expense is taken into account. For non-common law countries the same considerations do not apply.[3] Where there is a single alien system of law the only criterion by which the Privy Council appeal can be judged is the actual comparative competence of the Judicial Committee and of the court appealed from in the particular system of law concerned. This is a matter for the enlightened judgment of practitioners and scholars in that particular doctrine. Where, as in India, there is a multiplicity of communal laws, the Judicial Committee may well be in a better position than any local court of appeal to weld them by insensible steps into a coherent body of law.

We have shown above that unless a Dominion is seeking to break, but has not yet definitely broken, with the formal unity of Empire

England. Canada and Australia, the largest in population, are each split, for most purposes of private law and jurisdiction, into several units.

[1] Cf. above, pp. 563, 569–70.

[2] For example, the unfortunate decisions of the Privy Council enumerated above, p. 566, are constantly cited in the High Court of Australia, which cannot escape feeling itself to some extent bound by them. For the canons of interpretation which the Privy Council has forced upon the Civil Code of Quebec, see Mr. Justice Mignault in 1 *University of Toronto Law Journal*, p. 104.

[3] There is a pale parallel to the function of the Privy Council for the common law in the case of Roman-Dutch law, where the existence of the Privy Council jurisdiction makes South African decisions authoritative in Ceylon, and vice versa.

law, there is no necessary connexion—and at the present time not even a fortuitous connexion—between the interpretation of Dominion constitutions in a nationalist sense and the final determination of constitutional appeals within Dominion borders. We have also seen that, so far as simple competence is concerned, there is no clear superiority of the Judicial Committee over the only Dominion court which now finally disposes of constitutional cases. The argument, so strong in private law, that unity of jurisdiction broadens and enriches the law of the countries partaking in it, has no force for constitutional law, for between the constitutional doctrines of the different Dominions there is now little common ground. There is therefore no reason why the lawyer should oppose any disposition of constitutional appeals which the dominant political forces in his Dominion—whether they are nationalist, imperialist, or provincialist —may desire. But he can and should demand that, whatever court is chosen, it should hear all constitutional appeals from the Dominion without exception. The arbitrary division of the Australian field between the High Court and the Privy Council has been nothing but an embarrassment to both.[1] But the distinction between constitutional questions and private law is not hard to draw, and there is no reason why the political forces which will inevitably determine the disposal of constitutional appeals should touch the unifying influence of the Privy Council in private law, to which they are not relevant.

NOTES

Analytical Tables concerning the Business of the Judicial Committee from Michaelmas Term 1934 to Trinity Term 1936

These figures relate not to all cases heard during the period, but to cases in which judgments were delivered within the period. Consolidated appeals are treated as single cases.

I. Size of Boards at Hearing

Number of cases heard by Boards of :	Five	Four	Three	Total
Dominion Appeals	21	2	9	32
Channel Islands and Northern Ireland cases	2	..	1	3
Colonial Appeals	2	..	30	32
Indian Appeals	15	..	98	113
All cases	40	2	138	180

[1] The Royal Commission on the Constitution of the Commonwealth, 1929, recommended that all constitutional questions should be finally determined by the High Court: Report, p. 254.

II. *Provenance of Appeals*

Dominion Appeals:

Canada (Federal courts 6, provincial courts 12)	18
Australia (High Court 5, State Supreme Courts 3) . . .	8
New Zealand	5
Irish Free State	1

Total Dominion Appeals	32

Channel Island Appeals and Northern Ireland
Constitutional References **3**

Appeals from Colonies, Mandates, Protectorates, &c.:

Mediterranean (Gibraltar, Malta, Palestine)	5
Asiatic (Ceylon, Malaya, Hong Kong)	8
African (East and West)	9
American (West Indies and British Honduras) . . .	8
Pacific (Fiji)	2

Total Colonial Appeals	32

Indian Appeals (including Burma)   .   .   .   . | 113

TOTAL	180

The unit in the two succeeding tables is each occasion upon which each individual member takes his seat to hear a case.

III. *National Origins of Privy Councillors Sitting*

	Dominion Appeals (32)	Chan. Is. and N.I. (3)	Colonial Appeals (32)	Indian Appeals (113)	All Cases (180)
Members and ex-members of the English* judiciary (11) . .	81	8	73	87	249
Members and ex-members of the Scottish* judiciary (4) . .	34	3	16	84	137
Anglo-Indian ex-members of the Indian legal service (4) . .	12	2	10	123 ⎫	213
Indian ex-members of the Indian legal service (1) . . .	..	..	..	66 ⎭	
Dominion judges (4) . .	4	..	..	1	5

* Lords of Appeal in Ordinary are appointed for the United Kingdom as a whole. They are here allocated to the countries of their professional careers.

IV. *Classes of Privy Councillors Sitting*

	Dominion Appeals (32)	Chan. Is. and N.I. (3)	Colonial Appeals (32)	Indian Appeals (113)	All Cases (180)
Lord Chancellor (1) . . .	6	2	3	..	11
Ex-Lord Chancellor (1) . .	2	..	..	..	2
Lords of Appeal in Ordinary and Master of the Rolls (9) . .	86	6	57	140	289
Ex-judges of English and Scottish courts (4) . . .	21	3	29	31	84
Members appointed for India (salaried) (5). . . .	12	2	10	189	213
Dominion judges (4) . .	4	..	..	1	5

3. *Fundamental Rules of the Commonwealth Association*

The first section of this chapter ended upon a distinction within the general law of the Empire between ordinary law and fundamental law. To speak of an imperial fundamental law may seem strange. For fundamental law in general jurisprudence means law which is not alterable by ordinary legislation, but only by some more difficult process, if at all; and it is a platitude that the British Parliament can change any law by ordinary legislation and cannot deprive itself of the freedom so to do. (It has been argued above,[1] it is true, that every system of law, even the British one, must have a *Grundnorm*, and a *Grundnorm* is by definition fundamental law; but the British *Grundnorm* is a very little one, and for most practical purposes the traditional doctrine is as nearly true as makes no difference.) To the extent that the technical legal supremacy of the Imperial Parliament is recognized—and, as we have seen, it is recognized everywhere in the Empire except in the Irish Free State and, possibly, South Africa—how can there be any talk of fundamental law in the Empire?

So long as legislation at Westminster is regarded as the *ordinary* process of legislation for all the Empire, the criticism is just. But since the very beginning of colonial constitutions, it has not been so regarded. For any colony which has local legislative institutions, the ordinary process of legislation is the local process. All law which cannot be changed by local legislation is therefore, from the colonial point of view, fundamental. The relation in which local legislation stands to such law is essentially the same relation as that in which

---

[1] Section II (1).

the statutes of the United States Congress stand to the Constitution of the United States.

In a colony or Dominion, though not in the United States, it is possible to distinguish two elements in the law which is called fundamental. Some (or all) of it is removed from colonial legislative control in order that the imperial supremacy over the colony may be maintained; there may also be (though there is not always) law which has fundamental status simply in order that the rigidity in certain respects of the colonial constitution may be ensured. The distinction is a purely political one, and in the case of a definitely subordinate colony it cannot be drawn with accuracy. Who can say, for example, how far the delimitation of the respective spheres of legislature and executive in Sierra Leone is directed merely to the efficient working of the domestic government of that colony, and how far to the maintenance of imperial control? But the distinction grows in political importance and in precision as the measure of colonial autonomy increases, and modern constitutional doctrine has for some time recognized a vital distinction between, for example, the provisions in the British North America Act which deal with the constitution and the powers of the Canadian provincial legislatures and the clauses in the Act of Settlement, 1701, laying down the succession to the Crown. Both affect Canada, and both have binding force there. Both are fundamental law there, that is to say, they are alterable only by Act of the Imperial Parliament. But a change in the former is recognized as concerning Canada alone, and the Imperial Parliament in amending the British North America Act in such respects now limits its discretion to ascertaining whether the wishes of Canada, both provinces and Dominion, concur in demanding the amendment; a change in the latter concerns the Empire as a whole, and Canada as a part of it. It is convenient to speak of the former as local fundamental law and the latter as imperial fundamental law.

Imperial fundamental law is, however, not the only or even the chief element in the rules which govern the Commonwealth association. The basis of the modern Commonwealth relationship is equality, but the intractable Austinianism of British legal theory makes it incapable of recognizing a relationship which is fundamentally equalitarian. Imperial fundamental law, in the sense defined above, is fundamental for the Dominions, but not for the United Kingdom, since the United Kingdom Parliament, the ordinary legislature of Great Britain, may in law repeal any part of it at pleasure. To redress this inequality that body of doctrine which is called Commonwealth convention has been called in. It operates in two ways: by hindering the United Kingdom from altering certain rules of law which are essential to the Commonwealth, and by facilitating the alteration at the instance of the Dominions of laws which, though not essential to the Commonwealth, have still fundamental status. A typical convention of the first type is the limitation of the supremacy of the Imperial Parliament by the recital in the Statute of Westminster that 'no law hereafter made by the Parliament of the United Kingdom shall extend to any of the . . . Dominions as part of the law of that Dominion otherwise than at the request and with the consent of that Dominion'. A typical convention of the second type is that which obliges the Imperial Parliament to make any amendment of the British North America Act which is requested by the Dominion of Canada and all the Provinces. There are, of course, other Commonwealth conventions which are not concerned with redressing inequalities of law.

It is easy to draw a distinction between ordinary and fundamental Commonwealth conventions analogous to that already drawn between ordinary and fundamental imperial law. Those conventions which are inalterable except by the common consent of members of the Commonwealth may properly be described as fundamental to the Commonwealth association. But it is hard to say precisely which among the many conventional obligations between members of the Commonwealth bear this character. The test of the fundamental quality of law is easy: legislation in breach of it is invalid, and will be so held by the courts. But convention consists, by definition, of rules not enforceable in courts of law, and so cannot invalidate law. Since, however, the Commonwealth is in convention a voluntary association,[1] it may be said that the sanction for breach of fundamental convention is exclusion from the Commonwealth association. But even this is not sufficiently precise, for the Commonwealth association is notoriously elastic, and things are now tolerated and approved in Dominions which not long ago would have been thought quite incompatible with imperial loyalty. There is, then, no sure test of the fundamental quality of a Commonwealth convention other than the behaviour of the Commonwealth as a whole when confronted with a breach of it, and that is not predictable with any accuracy. The only guide to its prediction is the prevalent opinion concerning the essentials of the Commonwealth, and it must be recognized that this opinion differs from Dominion to Dominion, and between

[1] Its members are 'freely associated': *Balfour Report*, Cmd. 2768, p. 14.

Great Britain and certain Dominions. There is, however, a sufficient consensus of opinion to establish certain conventions as fundamental.

The development of the Commonwealth into a voluntary association has changed the practical, though not the technical, significance of the imperial part of its fundamental law. It is still technically true that an act done in breach of fundamental law has no legal effect, for the sanction of all fundamental law is invalidity. Acts done *ultra vires* are, in the eye of the law, not done at all; and if the person doing them is anything but a natural person (i.e. an individual human being), it simply does not exist, in the eye of the law, to do anything but what it is authorized to do. When the political institutions of the colonies were first set up, these technical doctrines were in a certain sense parallel to the facts, for their constitutions were not intended to be the framework of a generally competent political organism, but only to exercise certain selected powers. But those institutions became in fact political frameworks for nations, the reality of whose nationhood transcended the institutions of its origin. The imperial acts which set up the constitutions of the various Dominions are rightly no longer regarded in the Dominions as the sole or even the principal ground of the existence in fact of their national identity and national institutions. The meaning of a legal institution cannot be assessed apart entirely from its practical social significance. In practice, observance of imperial fundamental law is not now for the Dominions a condition precedent to their national existence, but an obligation incident to their membership, as nations, of a voluntary association of nations, the British Commonwealth. This is true equally of the Dominions that have and of those that have not asserted local roots for their systems of law—indeed, the mere fact that such assertions have been possible is a testimony to the change.

Observance of imperial fundamental law being now for practical purposes an obligation upon nations incident to their membership of the Commonwealth, it is not easily distinguishable in function from fundamental Commonwealth convention, which bore that character from its beginning. There are only two differences, one of which gives law a higher efficacy than convention, the other a lower. In the Dominions which still form part of the formal imperial system of law, acts done in breach of imperial fundamental law are necessarily void in Dominion domestic law, whereas fundamental Commonwealth convention lacks this sanction of nullity. On the other hand, just because convention creates not literal obligations of law but vague obligations of a moral or political quality, its requirements may be less easily evaded by fulfilment of the letter and neglect of the spirit than the requirements of strict law.[1]

The tendency towards assimilation of imperial fundamental law to convention has had opposite incidental effects on local fundamental law in the Dominions which have preponderantly rigid and preponderantly flexible constitutions respectively. The two great federations have inevitably each a large *corpus* of domestic fundamental law, which they have had to preserve in full force in order that their federal character may not be destroyed. The frequent application of this law by the courts to invalidate statutes and executive acts has saved it from any sort of atrophy, and it has been expressly excepted from the operation of the Statute of Westminster for both Canada and Australia.[2]

In South Africa, on the other hand, where there was no element of rigidity in the domestic constitution except the relatively unimportant 'entrenched clauses' of the South Africa Act, the emancipatory effect of the Statute of Westminster has been allowed to extend to them as well.[3] The position in the Irish Free State is obscure. There are two possible sources of rigidity for Free State constitutional law: the Treaty and the Constitution. The Constitution is made fundamental law by its own Article 2, and the sanction of judicial review is provided by Article 65. Amendments may, by Article 50, only be made by the Oireachtas with the assent in a referendum of either the absolute majority of the registered voters or a two-thirds majority of those voting. But this article is made subject to a proviso that for the first eight years it may be amended by ordinary legislation. Under this proviso an amendment was passed in 1929[4] extending the duration of the operation of the proviso itself to sixteen years, and this amendment was held valid in *State (Ryan)* v. *Lennon*.[5] Accordingly the Constitution strictly so called of the Irish Free State is for the moment completely flexible, but it may be rendered rigid by amendment,[6] and in the absence

[1] See, e.g. the then Commonwealth Attorney-General in the Australian House of Representatives, 17th July 1931 (Keith, *Speeches and Documents on the British Dominions, 1918–1931*, pp. 264–5).

[2] In slightly different terms for each. See below, p. 589.

[3] Kennedy and Schlosberg, *Law and Custom of the South African Constitution*, pp. 100, 101.

[4] Constitution (Amendment No. 16) Act, No. 10 of 1929.

[5] 1935 I.R. 170.

[6] In this respect it is similar not to the British constitution but to the constitutions of those colonies and States which are governed by s. 5 of the Colonial Laws Validity Act 1865: *Attorney-General for New South Wales* v. *Trethowan*, [1932] A.C. 526.

of further amendment will automatically become rigid in 1938.[1] At the time of writing, an extensive recasting of the Constitution[2] is foreshadowed by the Free State Government.

The flexibility or otherwise of the Constitution strictly so called does not as such touch the Treaty, which was declared by section 2 of the Constituent Act[3] to have a force superior to any provision of the Constitution or amendment to the Constitution, and whose provisions were excepted from the power of amendment given by Article 50 of the Constitution.   In 1933 an amendment of the Constitution repealing these limitations was passed,[4] and in 1935 a subsequent amendment of the Constitution[5] inconsistent with the Treaty was held valid in Irish Free State domestic law by the Privy Council.[6] But since the Privy Council has no longer jurisdiction in Irish appeals, its view is not binding on Free State Courts, and in fact there are dicta of the Free State Supreme Court in the earlier decision of *State (Ryan)* v. *Lennon*[7] tending to the opposite view. It may, however, be surmised that the Supreme Court will not regard the Treaty as fundamental if ever a square decision on the point is required of it.[8]

In short, the weakening of imperial fundamental law by the

[1] Lord Justice Greene suggests to the writer that on the view of the Statute of Westminster taken by the Judicial Committee in *Moore* v. *Attorney-General of the Irish Free State*, [1935] A.C. 484, the Constitution would remain amendable by ordinary legislative process after the expiry of the second eight-year period by virtue of the power which the Statute confers to amend imperial acts, the Constitution being part of an imperial act. This is a power quite separate from, and independent of, the amending power contained in Art. 50. But it is unlikely that the Irish courts will take the view that the Imperial Parliament is capable of conferring *ab extra* any such power on the Oireachtas.

[2] Beyond the Constitution (Amendment No. 27) Act, No. 57 of 1936, which was passed at the time of King Edward VIII's abdication. For its effect see below, p. 586, n. 2.

[3] Scheduled to 13 Geo. 5, c. 1.

[4] Constitution (Removal of Oath) Act, No. 6 of 1933.

[5] Constitution (Amendment No. 22) Act, No. 45 of 1933.

[6] *Moore* v. *Attorney-General of the Irish Free State*, [1935] A.C. 484; 1935 I.R. 472.

[7] [1935] I.R. 170. Fitzgibbon, J., at p. 227, states firmly that amendments inconsistent with the Treaty would be void; Murnaghan, J., the other member of the majority, countenances this view without expressly affirming it; the view of Kennedy, C.J., who dissented, is difficult to ascertain from his dicta at pp. 205–7, but seems to tend in the same direction. The effect of the Statute of Westminster, which was the sole ground of the Privy Council decision, is not adverted to in any of the judgments of the Supreme Court.

[8] If the Supreme Court were to declare the Treaty still fundamental, the Constitution (Amendment No. 27) Act, No. 57 of 1936, which removes the Governor-General from the Constitution, would almost certainly be invalid. All legislation passed since that Act would therefore be invalid, not having been signed by the Governor-General.

Statute of Westminster and by the assertion of local roots for
Dominion systems of law has had the effect in unitary Dominions
of weakening or eliminating rigid elements in the local constitutions.
In the two federal Dominions, on the other hand, it has accentuated
the difference between imperial and local fundamental law, the latter
being preserved in full force.

It remains to state the fundamental rules of the Commonwealth
association as it now is, and to estimate how far they are properly
described as rules of convention, how far as rules of law. We have
already suggested that fundamental Commonwealth convention
must, from its subjective character, necessarily be vague. Some
even question whether its provisions are sufficiently binding to be
properly classed as rules at all. It is true that nearly all the standards
which, politically speaking, imperialists consider essential have been
infringed by the Irish Free State, and each infringement has been in
greater or lesser degree condoned by the United Kingdom and the
other members of the Commonwealth. Yet the principal unques-
tionable breaches of convention by the Free State[1] have been
breaches not of general Commonwealth convention at all, but of
the Anglo-Irish Treaty. This agreement certainly has, amongst other
qualities, the quality of convention as between the parties to it; but
it was concluded before the generalization of the conventions of
Dominion status in 1926 first established the general character of the
Commonwealth as a voluntary association of equals, and thereby first
rendered conventions fundamental to the association possible.
Breaches of the Treaty are accordingly merely breaches of a private
bilateral 'contractual'[2] arrangement, not of the multilateral fundamental conventions establishing the status of a member of the
Commonwealth as such.

That objection set aside, there seems no reason why the conventions stated in the Balfour Memorandum, with proper allowance for
its slightly exalted language, should not be taken seriously as rules
still regulating the conduct of Commonwealth affairs.

None of them are stated in so many words to be fundamental or
to require common consent to their alteration. But in the crucial

---

[1] Exceptions are the introduction of the Bill for the Irish Nationality and Citizenship Act, 1935, without prior consultation, contrary to the Report of the 1930
Imperial Conference (Cmd. 3717, p. 22), and Mr. De Valera's ambiguous remarks in
the Dáil on 11 December 1936. Mr. D. L. Keir rightly observes to the writer that
even those breaches which break only a bilateral arrangement have nevertheless a
deteriorating effect on the standing of Commonwealth convention generally.

[2] The Privy Council used this epithet in *Moore's Case*, [1935] A.C. 484, 499.

definition the members of the Commonwealth are said to be 'united by a common allegiance to the Crown'. It is hard to think that a member could remain a member if it utterly disavowed the common Crown. The 1930 Conference certainly interpreted one aspect of this requirement as fundamental when it laid down the corollary, afterwards recited for emphasis in the preamble to the Statute of Westminster, that

> 'it would be in accord with the established constitutional position of all the members of the Commonwealth in relation to one another that any alteration in the law touching the Succession to the Throne or the Royal Style and Titles shall hereafter require the assent as well of the Parliaments of all the Dominions as of the Parliament of the United Kingdom.'

On the only occasion which has hitherto arisen for its application, namely, the abdication of King Edward VIII and the institution of King George VI in 1936, this convention has worked, though not without creaking. The Australian Parliament was the only one to express its assent before His Majesty's Declaration of Abdication Act was passed at Westminster. The Dáil did not in so many words express its assent to the passing of the Act, but passed legislation making what amounts to an identical change in the succession, which came into effect on the following day. The other Dominion *parliaments* expressed their assent in various ways within the next few months. The change in the succession came into effect in all of them, except the Irish Free State, at the same time as in Great Britain; in Australia and New Zealand (which have not adopted the Statute) by virtue of the overriding force of imperial legislation under the Colonial Laws Validity Act, 1865; in Canada by virtue of the request and consent of the Canadian Government recited in the Act pursuant to section 4 of the Statute of Westminster; and in South Africa by virtue of section 3 of the South Africa Act, which defines the King in South Africa as the King for the time being under the laws of the United Kingdom.[1] The ancillary conventions governing the tendering of advice to the Crown in matters touching the succession are clearly not fundamental, for they were broken in 1936 by the governments of the United Kingdom and (possibly) the Irish Free State without impairing the Commonwealth association.[2]

[1] The text, which represents a view to which the writer still adheres, was written before His Majesty King Edward VIII's Abdication Bill was introduced into the Union Parliament. This Bill declares the abdication to have taken effect immediately upon the signing of the Instrument of Abdication, on 10 December. See below, p. 618.

[2] A more detailed account of the abdication in imperial constitutional law is given in the Appendix, below, pp. 616–30.

Concerning nationality, though there is, as we shall see, an indelible but impotent common status in fundamental law,[1] there is no fundamental convention, despite the reference in the Balfour Memorandum to a 'common allegiance' as the basis of Commonwealth unity. Grammatically, the allegiance there referred to is that of the 'communities' of the Commonwealth, not that of their citizens. But in any case, there was in 1926 no 'common allegiance', in the strict sense, of the citizens of all the member nations of the Commonwealth, because even at that time the incidents attached to allegiance in the Dominions were widely different, and the classes of persons regarded by the various Dominions as within that allegiance did not exactly coincide. There is no doubt, however, that the duty of maintaining the largest possible measure of effective common or mutual citizenship is one of the principal non-fundamental conventions of the Commonwealth.[2]

It is probable that there is another fundamental convention of the Commonwealth, not mentioned in the Balfour Memorandum: a rule that the admission of a new member of the Commonwealth requires the consent of all. This may seem startling, for the last member of the Commonwealth to be admitted—the Irish Free State, in 1921— was admitted by the sole authority of the United Kingdom, as all others had previously been. But the rule follows logically from the equal and consequently multilateral character of the Commonwealth relationship established in 1926.[3] Equality precludes the possibility that any one member of the Commonwealth should have the exclusive prerogative of admitting new members. Therefore, either new members can be admitted by any member acting alone, or they can only be admitted by common consent of all. Clearly, the admission of a foreign nation would require the consent of all. The admission of territories already within the Empire which have not previously been fully self-governing in every aspect of their internal and external affairs, whether they are dependencies of a member of the Commonwealth (e.g. India and Southern Rhodesia) or whether they form part of the domestic territory of a member of the Commonwealth (e.g. Western Australia, Quebec, Scotland) would raise difficult questions. Of course, complete self-governing status (in fact if not in form) is a pre-requisite for membership, and this can only be accorded by the member of the Commonwealth of which the candidate is a dependency

[1] Below, pp. 592–5.
[2] Report of Conference on the Operation of Dominion Legislation and Merchant Shipping, paras. 72–9, Cmd. 3479 of 1929, pp. 24–5; Report of 1930 Imperial Conference, section VI (b), Cmd. 3717, pp. 21–2.
[3] For the multilateral character of the modern Commonwealth, see below, pp. 597–8.

or a part. But when it has been accorded, does it *ipso facto* confer Commonwealth membership, without the consent of the other members ? It is submitted that, in principle, their consent is necessary. This is so not because the present members of the Commonwealth have any sort of monopoly of status, but because the accession of a new member would render the general conventions of the Commonwealth automatically applicable between it and the existing members. This would amount to an extension of the conventional obligations of existing members, and as such it would require their consent.[1] But in practice this principle must, it would seem, be qualified by the consideration that in accepting—and indeed welcoming—the presence of Southern Rhodesian and Indian representatives at imperial conferences expressly in anticipation of their future full status in the Commonwealth, the present members of the Commonwealth must be taken to have consented in advance to their admission to the Commonwealth as soon as they shall have been granted full autonomy by the United Kingdom. The same argument would apply *a fortiori* to the restitution of Newfoundland to full Dominion status.[2]

These are the fundamental conventions of the Commonwealth association. There remain two other sorts of Commonwealth convention. There are those positive conventions of the Commonwealth association which are not fundamental, the chief of which are those concerning foreign affairs. These are of all conventions the most significant of the true nature of the Commonwealth relationship, but they do not touch the present topic. There are also those negative and supplementary conventions of Dominion status which fill up the remaining inequalities in law between the United Kingdom and the Dominions to an effective practical equality of status. It was once the main task of the constitutional student of the Empire to enunciate these conventions separately, and estimate how far each had gone in the direction of complete emancipation. But it is now not only easier but more accurate simply to state that the Dominions have in convention complete equality of status according to the definition in the Balfour Memorandum. All conventions necessary to implement that status are implied. The extent of the conventions so implied corresponds exactly with the extent of the remaining in-

---

[1] It is true that the Report of the Committee of Both Houses on the Receivability of the Petition of Western Australia for Secession (Parl. Pap. 1935, H.C. 88) asserted only that the consent of the Commonwealth of Australia would be necessary to legislation erecting the State of Western Australia into a separate Dominion. But the question of the consent of the other Dominions was not raised, and the absence in fact of the consent of the Australian government was sufficient to dispose of the matter.   [2] See above, p. 526, n. 4.

equality in strict law. Some of the conventions of this class will of necessity be mentioned in the ensuing account of imperial fundamental law.

In stating the imperial fundamental law of the present day it is necessary to consider not only the extent of its provisions, but also the derivation of, and the security for, its fundamental character. In both these respects it has been debilitated by modern developments: in its extent by legislation, principally the Statute of Westminster, and in its fundamental character by the assertion of local roots for Dominion systems of law.

The effective assertion of a local root for the law of a Dominion has two quite separate effects on the application of imperial fundamental law to that Dominion. In the first place, it removes from the law of that Dominion the theoretical possibility that any or all of the laws of the Dominion might at any time be overborne by imperial legislation. In the second place, it definitely separates imperial fundamental law from local fundamental law. Thus there is translated into legal theory the political distinction which we have drawn between imperial and local fundamental law, and also the change in the function of imperial fundamental law which we have mentioned above, whereby from being the ground of the national existence of the Dominion it has become merely the embodiment of some of the terms of the Dominion's membership of a voluntary association, the Commonwealth. It may retain fundamental status in the Dominion, so that ordinary legislation repugnant to it is void; but if it does, it enjoys that status no longer in virtue of logical priority to (or at least parity with) the local fundamental law, but in virtue of its adoption by the latter, in the same manner as international treaties are by the United States Constitution[1] adopted into American law.

The institution of the Crown and the law of succession to it as enacted by the Parliament of the United Kingdom are still fundamental law in each of the Dominions, except the Irish Free State.[2] This exception, however, does not disprove the rule, because of the

---

[1] Art. 6. 2.

[2] Art. 51 of the Free State Constitution, as amended by the Constitution (Amendment No. 27) Act, No. 57 of 1936, provides only that any 'organ' used as a constitutional organ for the appointment of diplomatic and consular agents and the conclusion of international agreements by any of the nations of the Commonwealth may be availed of by the Free State Executive Council for those purposes 'to the extent and subject to any conditions which may be determined by law' (i.e. by ordinary legislation). Pursuant to this provision, the King recognized by the Commonwealth nations 'as the symbol of their co-operation' is by the Executive Authority (External

anomalous nature of the Free State's membership of the Commonwealth. Imperial fundamental law requires that the monarch remain,
in name at least, head of the executive throughout the Empire. Are
any inalienable powers coupled with this headship, or is it wholly
nominal? Apart from the Statute of Westminster, the Crown retains
in law all those prerogatives in relation to the Dominions which are
not vested in the Governors-General and Governors by the Dominion
constitutions or delegated to them by royal instructions; and, apart
from power expressly given in the constitutions, Dominion parliaments cannot derogate from these retained powers. The exact limits
of these powers has long been a matter of dispute, and their determination has been rendered unnecessary in practice by the establishment of conventions that, whatever their extent may be, they are
exercisable only on the advice of Dominion ministers, so that in fact
Dominion cabinets exercise all executive power in relation to their
Dominions, whether it is legally vested in the Governor-General or in
the monarch in person. The question how far the King's prerogative
is incapable of being taken from him by Dominion statute therefore
loses much, though not all, of its importance. Not all, because circumstances are conceivable in which a monarch might disregard his
conventional duty to a Dominion in which he was not resident, particularly if the performance of that duty should be inconsistent with
his conventional duty to another member of the Commonwealth,
as it would be if the advice of their cabinets on a common matter
were to conflict.

The common matters, in which the King cannot act differently for
different parts of the Empire, but must do a single act for all, include
on the one hand matters concerning his life as an individual, such as
his marriage and his bodily locomotion (for he cannot be corporally
partitioned among the members of the Commonwealth),[1] and on the
other hand matters in which his function is deemed to be indivisible
by imperial fundamental law. Issues of peace and war have usually
been regarded as belonging to the latter category. Actually, the
states of belligerency and neutrality, though by a compendious
metaphor they are spoken of as attributes or conditions of states or
heads of states, are significant principally in their application to
nationals of those states. The real juristic difficulty in regarding the

Relations) Act, No. 58 of 1936, authorized to act for the Free State in such matters
when advised by the Executive Council. There is now no other mention of the King
in the Constitution. The King is accordingly eliminated from the internal affairs
of the Free State.

[1] See the Appendix (below, p. 616) for a discussion of some of the conventions,
fundamental and otherwise, touching the monarch's personal life.

Commonwealth as divisible in matters of peace and war lies not in any supposed indivisibility of the Crown in this respect—for the Crown, like any other fictitious entity, exists only to have arbitrary meanings given to it—but in the extreme difficulty of distinguishing in such matters between the nationals of one member of the Commonwealth and those of another, so long as and to the extent that the status of British subject is for these purposes the common nationality of the citizens of all members of the Commonwealth.

The only provisions of the Statute of Westminster which affect the power of the Dominions to deprive the Crown of its prerogatives, namely sections 2 and 3, appear at first sight to many orthdox lawyers to do no more than free Dominion legislation which is otherwise *intra vires* from two general restrictions which had hitherto been imposed on it apart from the limits contained in the original grant of power: the restriction (whatever it may be) on extra-territorial effect, and invalidity for repugnancy to imperial Acts expressly or by necessary implication extending to the Dominions. The abolition of an external limitation on a granted power does not enlarge the grant itself. On this view, these sections would not enable the Dominion Parliaments to affect matters, such as royal prerogatives of an imperial, not a local character, which the law had hitherto simply deemed not to be included in the original grants of legislative power to the Dominions.[1] But a less literal view of the effect of those sections prevailed in *British Coal Corporation* v. *R.*[2] and *Moore* v. *Attorney-General for the Irish Free State.*[3] These cases establish that sections 2 and 3 are to be construed as an independent grant of power. It is impossible now to say what are the legal limits to the powers of those Dominion Parliaments which take the full benefit of these sections of the Statute. It seems unlikely that any measure circumscribing the powers of the Crown in such Dominions, however radically, would now be held invalid. There is, then, probably nothing in imperial fundamental law to prevent those Dominions (i.e. the Union of South Africa and the Irish Free State) from legislating to deprive the monarch of every power and dignity except his bare status as monarch and perhaps his established royal style and titles.[4]

The precise extent of the additional powers which the Statute has

---

[1] See Dean V. C. MacDonald in 13 *Can. Bar. Rev.* 625, and Mr. Justice Dixon in 10 *Aust. Law Journ., Supp.* 96.

[2] [1935] A.C. 500.   [3] [1935] A.C. 484.

[4] Instances of Dominion legislation regulating the Crown's prerogatives in a radical way are the Status of the Union Act, No. 69 of 1934 (South Africa) and the Constitution (Amendment No. 27) Act, No. 57 of 1936 (Irish Free State) with which must be read the Royal Executive Functions and Seals Act, No. 70 of 1934 (South

conferred upon the Canadian and will, if fully adopted, confer on the New Zealand and Australian Commonwealth legislatures, is uncertain. The section[1] saving the Constitutions of Australia and New Zealand probably prohibits only legislation which alters those instruments textually or declares rules for their construction, and imposes no obstacle to legislation by the Dominion parliaments outside the powers conferred on them by the Constitutions, under the new powers conferred by sections 2 and 3 as now broadly construed.[2] The section saving the British North America Act, however, provides further that the additional powers conferred on Dominion and provincial legislatures shall not extend beyond the subject-matters at present allotted to the competence of each.[3] The benefit of the Statute extends to the legislatures of the Canadian provinces, but not to the Parliaments of the Australian States. It seems probable, then, that the New Zealand parliament and, in relation to federal matters, the Australian Commonwealth parliament would have, on adopting the Statute, as full power to minimize the royal office as the Irish and South African legislatures have, but that the State Parliaments in Australia have gained no new freedom in this respect.[4] The decision in *British Coal Corporation* v. *R.*[5] suggests that the powers of both federal and provincial legislatures in Canada to limit the royal prerogative have been considerably increased by the Statute. It cannot therefore be said with certainty that in the remaining Dominions the royal powers are any better protected from the inroads of Dominion legislation than they are in South Africa and the Irish Free State.

Canada, Australia, and New Zealand have in fact taken no steps derogating from the powers or dignity of the imperial Crown, unless Canada's abolition of the Privy Council appeal in criminal cases can be so regarded. Indeed, the change in the position of the Governor-General which was effected at the 1926 Conference, whereby he became in theory the direct personal representative of the Crown, and not at all of the British government (this does not yet apply in New Zealand) increased, nominally at least, the intimacy of the connexion between the Crown and the Dominions, though in fact the right which Dominion governments acquired at the same time to be

Africa) and the Executive Authority (External Relations) Act, No. 58 of 1936 (Irish Free State) respectively.
    [1] s. 8.   [2] Cf. Dixon, op. cit., p. 99.   [3] s. 7.
    [4] The Commonwealth Parliament's power would probably include even the regulation of matters now regulated by Imperial act which are of purely State concern, provided only that they are not 'within the authority of a State'. Dixon, op. cit., p. 101.   [5] [1935] A.C. 500.

the exclusive advisers of the Crown in the appointment of Governors-General has as often as not been exercised with more regard to the closeness of the appointee's connexion with the Dominion than to his personal acquaintance with the monarch. The Irish Free State first minimized the dignity of the Crown in the Free State by appointing as its representative a nonentity who merely signed documents, and then, in 1936, eliminated it entirely from the internal constitution of the Free State, though retaining it for Commonwealth affairs.[1] South Africa has, on the other hand, done nothing to detract from the dignity of the Crown, but has effectively nullified the personal power of the King by statutorily empowering the Governor-General to act on his behalf in practically all circumstances.[2]

Imperial fundamental law is, then, no effective safeguard for common monarchical institutions in the Commonwealth. Convention is a somewhat better safeguard; but the real assurance of the continuance of the monarchy lies in two political facts: the strength of the monarchical tradition and the difficulty which would be experienced in adjusting the form of the Commonwealth association to any other kind of régime.

From the consideration of the Privy Council appeal above[3] it appears that the appeal now figures very little, if at all, in imperial fundamental law.

The most important matter in imperial fundamental law is the legislative supremacy of the Imperial Parliament. In the last analysis, this supremacy is absolute for Dominions belonging to the imperial system of law, since for them the imperial parliament may validly repeal even the Statute of Westminster, and non-existent for Dominions which treat their law as having local roots, since in their view any legislative functions which the imperial parliament exercises for them it exercises merely by the authority or at the sufferance of the local Constitution or legislature.[4] Since, however, the repeal of the Statute is not a practical possibility to be reckoned with, it is desirable to estimate what powers to pass legislation for the Dominions unrepealable by Dominion parliaments the imperial parliament has while the Statute stands. There is a general power under s. 4

---

[1] Constitution (Amendment No. 27) Act, No. 57 of 1936, and the Executive Authority (External Relations) Act, No. 58 of 1936. See above, p. 586, n. 2. The precise effect of these enactments will take some time to become apparent. They were drafted and passed in a hurry, and will probably need further amendment.

[2] By the Royal Executive Functions and Seals Act, No. 70 of 1934.

[3] Pp. 550–2.

[4] Cf. the position with regard to amendment of the Irish Free State Constitution, see above, p. 581, n. 1.

of the Statute to legislate for the Dominions with the request and consent of the Dominion governments. Except for Australia, where the request and consent required are the request and consent of the Commonwealth parliament,[1] a Dominion government could under this section secure the enactment of an imperial statute over the head of its parliament—a power which might be useful to it in case of a conflict with an upper house. Such legislation would necessarily have the character of local rather than imperial fundamental law, because its repeal could be secured in the same manner as its enactment. It might, however, be rendered fundamental in convention if it were requested and consented to by all the Dominions, and a convention against unilateral repeal were set up analogous to the convention concerning the succession in the preamble to the Statute of Westminster. The present power of the imperial parliament to amend the British North America Act is fully preserved. It is in fact exercised according to strict conventions: no amendment affecting the provinces is passed without the consent of the provinces affected. The imperial parliament is, however, the judge whether or not an amendment requested by the Dominion alone does affect the provinces. The greater part of the local fundamental law in Australia is contained in the Commonwealth Constitution, which is amendable by a local process; but it is usually assumed that the 'covering clauses' (i.e. the first eight sections of the Commonwealth of Australia Constitution Act, 1900, of which the Constitution is section 9) are not amendable by that process.[2] Amendments of the terms of those clauses—and, possibly, amendments of the Constitution proper repugnant to those clauses[3]—must accordingly be made by imperial Act, and by section 8 of the Statute of Westminster the law and conventions touching such measures are preserved. There is little doubt that the same conventions which govern Canadian constitutional amendments govern such Australian amendments equally.[4]

The remaining topic of imperial fundamental law is nationality.

[1] s. 9 (3).
[2] So the Joint Committee on the Receivability of the Western Australia Secession Petition held (Parl. Pap. 1935, H.C. 88, Report, para. 6). But compare the opinion of Mr. Owen Dixon, K.C. (now Mr. Justice Dixon), printed as Appendix F to the Report of the Royal Commission on the Constitution, 1929, in which he holds that the federal nature of the Constitution could be validly destroyed by an amendment under s. 128, despite the reference in Covering Clause 3 to the Commonwealth as a 'Federal Commonwealth'. The ground for this view is presumably that the inability of the Commonwealth Parliament to amend the words of the covering clauses does not necessarily entail the invalidity of amendments which do not purport to amend those clauses but are in fact inconsistent with them. Cf. above, p. 589.
[3] On which see Mr. Justice Dixon, in 10 Aust. Law Journ., Supp. 99.
[4] Parl. Pap. 1935, H.C. 88, Report, para. 9.

There is in the modern Commonwealth a welter of nationalities, citizenships, and unnamed personal statuses which exist for a multitude of purposes. The various categories of 'citizenship' and 'nationality' created by dominion legislation can obviously be regulated in any way by dominion legislation, and so have no fundamental quality. Older than any of them is the status of British subject. The common law, and now the general provisions of the British Nationality and Status of Aliens Acts, 1914–22, which have been substituted for it, confer this status upon all persons born within the King's dominions[1] and a few born out of them, and provide that persons who have fulfilled certain requirements may acquire it by certificate of the Home Secretary of the United Kingdom or of a minister of a Dominion which has 'adopted' the Act.[2] The status so obtained is valid, for what it is worth, throughout the Empire, and must be distinguished from the status which a foreigner may acquire under Dominion Acts,[3] which can only be valid within the Dominion conferring it, and (since the Statute of Westminster at any rate) in relation to Dominion diplomatic and consular representatives abroad.

There is a common law rule of long standing that within its general legislative competence the legislature of every self-governing colony can regulate the *incidents or consequences* of the imperially valid status of British subject, but not the *status* itself.[4] This is still law. Prima facie, therefore, the *desiderata* for acquisition and loss of the imperially valid status of British subject, whether by birth, marriage, naturalization, or otherwise, are inalterable by Dominion legislation, and therefore constitute imperial fundamental law. But the legal significance of any status consists solely in its consequences in law. The imperially valid status of British subject is capable of having, and has in fact, consequences in law for its possessor in three spheres: in his own municipal[5] law, in the municipal laws of other parts of the Commonwealth, and in international law. We must therefore inquire to what extent its consequences in each of these spheres are guaranteed by imperial fundamental law.

The Canadian, the Australian, or the New Zealander enjoys his political rights and most other domestic rights of citizenship in his

---

[1] The King's dominions (which it is convenient to distinguish from the self-governing Dominions by the use of a small 'd') are all places which are under the Crown for the purposes of constitutional (not international) law. They do not include Protectorates or Mandated Territories.

[2] i.e. has adopted Part II of the British Nationality and Status of Aliens Act, 1914, pursuant to s. 9 thereof.

[3] For an account of this and other local statuses see *The British Empire*, chapter xx.

[4] See above, p. 520.   [5] See below, p. 595, n. 1.

Dominion in virtue of his status as a British subject. The Irishman or the South African, on the other hand, now enjoys these rights in his Dominion in virtue of his Irish citizenship or his South African nationality.[1] There is no doubt of the validity of the legislation which has created this state of affairs, and the other three Dominions could pass similar legislation if they wished.

Except in the Irish Free State,[2] the title by which some or all of the rights and duties of local citizenship are enjoyed by persons from other parts of the Commonwealth is their status as British subjects. But, clearly, a self-governing nation will extend privileges within its borders only to persons and categories of persons which it approves; nor, if it has decided by its law to accord or deny such privileges to a given person or category of persons, will it be restrained by any-thing in the law of the country of origin of these persons.[3] The legis-latures of the Dominions and Great Britain are therefore free, if they wish, to substitute other qualifications instead of the status of British subject as the title to such privileges, as the Irish Free State has already done.[2] No incidents of this kind, then, are attached to the status of British subject by imperial fundamental law.

The determination of the categories of persons to whom a diplo-matic or consular representative of Great Britain or a Dominion will accord protection is as much a function of the municipal law of the member of the Commonwealth which he serves as the determination of privileged categories in internal affairs.[4] Any doubt of the Domi-

[1] For accounts of Irish citizenship and South African nationality, see *The British Empire*, loc. cit. Not all British subjects are Irish citizens or South African nationals.

[2] In the Free State, most of the rights of citizenship are by the Aliens Order, 1935, extended not to British subjects as such, but to 'nationals or citizens' of Australia, Canada, Great Britain, South Africa, and New Zealand.

[3] Thus s. 33 of the Irish Nationality and Citizenship Act, No. 13 of 1935, provides that:

' (1) The British Nationality and Status of Aliens Act, 1914, and the British Nationality and Status of Aliens Act, 1918, if and so far as they respectively are or ever were in force in Saorstát Éireann, are hereby repealed.

(2) The common law relating to British nationality, if, and so far as it is, or ever was, either wholly or in part, in force in Saorstát Éireann, shall cease to have effect.

(3) The facts or events by reason of which a person is at any time a natural-born citizen of Saorstát Éireann shall not of themselves operate to confer on such person any other citizenship or nationality.'

But this enactment does not affect the law of the rest of the Commonwealth whereby Irishmen are British subjects, and are treated as such.

[4] The Irish Free State, however, by the Constitution (Amendment No. 27) Act, No. 57 of 1936 and the Executive Authority (External Relations) Act, No. 58 of 1936, empowers the Executive Council in future to advise the King in the appoint-ment of diplomatic and consular representatives. A representative appointed by the King for the United Kingdom with the advice or concurrence of the Free State Executive Council would thus be deemed in Irish law at least to protect Irish

nion's competence in this respect springing from the alleged territorial limitation of Dominion legislative power has been removed by section 3 of the Statute of Westminster.

It is indeed difficult to think of any incident or consequence in municipal law of the status of British subject[1] which is since the Statute of Westminster preserved from the control of the legislatures of the Dominions by imperial fundamental law.[2]

The question who may regulate the possession of the status of British subject in international law is quite another matter, and one of extreme obscurity. The suggestion may, however, be hazarded that if the Dominions which have erected categories of nationality of their own (i.e. Canada, South Africa, and the Irish Free State) were so to define these categories as to make them serviceable categories for the purposes of international law,[3] then, by reason of the undoubted international personality of these Dominions, a foreign nation would be justified in treating Dominion nationality as a true nationality for international purposes, and consequently applying the law of the Dominion, rather than any alleged imperial fundamental law conflicting with it, in determining whether or not a national of the Dominion had also the additional status of a British subject.[4] If this suggestion is correct, then the consequences in international law also of the status of British subject are controllable by Dominion legislatures.

It therefore seems likely that in law the consequences of that status of British subject whose acquisition is purported to be governed by imperial fundamental law are entirely malleable. So far as it confers rights and duties under the municipal laws of Commonwealth countries, those rights and duties are controlled by the relevant

citizens as such and by Irish authority. But if the Irish government or legislature should give him instructions incompatible with those given by the United Kingdom, he would doubtless follow the instructions of the government that paid him. No representative has yet been appointed in the manner contemplated. British representatives therefore continue to protect Irish citizens who are British subjects, by reason of their being British subjects, and Irish citizens who are not British subjects, by courtesy alone.

[1] The right of appeal to the Privy Council is not, as is often erroneously thought, a right attaching to British subjects as such, but extends to any party competent to bring or defend an action in a court from which the appeal lies.

[2] Some consequences may be prescribed by rigid constitutions, and thus be removed from the control of the legislature by *local* fundamental law; e.g., s. 23 of the British North America Act, 1867, requires Canadian senators to be British subjects.

[3] Dr. Baty, in 18 *Journ. Comp. Leg.* 195, 199 suggests that Canadian nationality is not yet serviceable in this respect. Irish Free State nationality, on the other hand, since the Irish Nationality and Citizenship Act, No. 13 of 1935, undoubtedly is.

[4] It is only in such circumstances that s. 33 (3) of the Irish Nationality and Citizenship Act, No. 13 of 1935 (quoted above, p. 593, n. 3) could have practical significance.

legislatures; so far as it confers a status in international law, the terms upon which that status may be acquired are controllable by the legislature of the member of the Commonwealth to which the relevant foreign power regards the person as primarily belonging. There is no certainty about it, but it is probably safer to deny than to assert that any rights or duties are firmly secured by imperial fundamental law to those upon whom it confers the name of British subject.

III

The Nature and Future of Commonwealth Obligation

A number of conventions, understandings, political practices and obligations, both general and particular, have come into existence to perform for the Commonwealth the function which is performed for centralized empires, for the most part, by constitutional law, and for the comity of nations, so far as it is performed at all, by international law—that is, to regulate the mutual relations of its members so far as they are capable of and require regulation by established and explicit rules. Neither municipal[1] law (of which constitutional law is an integral part) nor international law is merely a convenient descriptive classification of a number of essentially unrelated rules; both form more or less coherent systems—municipal law more, international law less. The question therefore arises whether the conventions, understandings, and obligations of the Commonwealth form likewise in any degree a coherent system, or are merely a congeries of rules connected only by a certain similarity of subject-matter. If they should be found to constitute a coherent system, the further question will arise, what is the relation of that system to municipal law on the one hand and international law on the other; and the possibility must not be excluded that Commonwealth conventions may prove to be or to have become indistinguishable from rules of municipal or of international law. These questions constitute at the moment a vital legal problem of the Commonwealth. It is a problem rich in theoretical interest and weighty with practical consequence, for upon the solution of it depends the possibility of establishing an effective tribunal which can guarantee the rule of some intelligible principle of order in Commonwealth affairs. The present essay does not assume or argue that Commonwealth affairs must be intelligibly ordered: there is virtue also in judicious disarray. It seeks only to

---

[1] By 'municipal law' international lawyers mean the system of law of each state, as distinct from international law. The word is used here in that sense.

examine what possible forms the rules of the Commonwealth might assume, if the Commonwealth is to be regulated by rules at all.

Where rules, whatever their origin, are administered in the same tribunal, and that tribunal operates fairly continuously, it will inevitably so interpret the rules as to make them cohere. In doing this, it treats them as belonging to a single system of law: and, as we have seen, courts in the English tradition are capable in practice of administering a system although its limits remain undefined and its *Grundnorm* shrouded in mystery. But there is no tribunal which has a general jurisdiction in Commonwealth convention, still less one in regular operation. The timid recommendation of the 1930 Imperial Conference in favour of *ad hoc* tribunals for Commonwealth disputes[1] has not once been applied, and in the only dispute in connexion with which its application was discussed, namely the Land Annuities dispute of 1932, the parties were unable to agree upon the composition of such a tribunal.[2] None of the tribunals which have actually taken cognizance of questions of Commonwealth convention has had any pretence to a general jurisdiction in that sphere. The Judicial Committee of the Privy Council considered and adjudged questions of convention in *British Coal Corporation* v. *R.*,[3] but only incidentally to its proper task, which lay in the sphere of strict law. The Joint Committee of the House of Lords and the House of Commons on the receivability of the Western Australian petition for secession from the Australian Commonwealth construed its task as extending to the ascertainment of the matters relevant to that issue and to that only, law being treated as ancillary and political merits neglected. Its report[4] is a valuable document in the authoritative literature of convention. But it was an *ad hoc* body, and acted solely under the authority and on behalf of the Parliament at Westminster.[5] Certain controversies between the India Office and the War Office concerning the liability of Indian revenues for the training of British troops for Indian service have indeed been dignified by the British Government with the appearance of a dispute between members of the Commonwealth, and an eminent Australian lawyer was called in to preside over the Tribunal which was set up in 1932 to advise on

[1] Cmd. 3717, pp. 23–5.   [2] Below, p. 607.   [3] [1935] A.C. 500. Below, pp. 613–14.
[4] *Parliamentary Papers*, 1935, H.L. 75, H.C. 88.
[5] Its members were Viscount Goschen (formerly Governor of Madras and for a short time Viceroy of India; with Australian experience); the Marquis of Lothian (formerly active in South African politics under Lord Milner; Secretary to the Rhodes Trust; imperial publicist), Lord Wright (Master of the Rolls, a law lord); Mr. L. C. M. S. Amery, M.P. (formerly Colonial and Dominions Secretary), Mr. Isaac Foot, M.P. (Solicitor), Mr. William Lunn, M.P. (formerly Parliamentary Under-Secretary for the Colonies and Dominions). Lord Goschen presided

the question. Its other members were two British and two Indian judges.[1] But India, not being self-governing, is a member of the Commonwealth only in an honorific and anticipatory sense,[2] and in any case the issue was not one of convention but of 'fair, just and equitable adjustment'.[3] There does not at present exist any jurisdiction which could conceivably of itself reduce Commonwealth convention to order and coherence. If it is a coherent system, or has a tendency towards coherence, that must spring from other causes and will be discernible from other considerations.

The distinction has already been drawn[4] between the conventions of status, which are rules inhibiting the operation of imperial institutions that are not in strict law equalitarian, and the conventions of co-operation, which have equality of status not as their end but as their basis. The former are mainly customary in origin. They operate on particular institutions such as the Crown, the United Kingdom cabinet, and the imperial parliament, imposing upon them in favour of Dominion freedom duties of abstention, and sometimes of action, over and above their duties in strict law. To a convention of this class there are normally only two parties: the Dominion interested and the imperial institution whose freedom is restricted. Conventions of co-operation may be customary, but are now more often contractual. The parties to them are the separate members of the Commonwealth regarded as political units, and they may be multilateral, like the general resolutions of imperial conferences, or bilateral, like the Ottawa agreements.

The early conventions of the self-governing colonies which were to become the Commonwealth were mostly, though not entirely, of the former, the inhibitory kind.[5] They developed from departmental and political practices which arose to meet particular needs. They bore no relation to each other beyond the resemblance of the circumstances in which they were conceived and the fact that many of them were administered by a single body, the Colonial Office. Formally, the degree of emancipation of each colony was a matter between it and the Colonial Office; there was no general status in convention which colonies, or colonies of a particular class, enjoyed as such. We can now see that the meeting of representatives of the colonies at

[1] The members were Sir Robert Garran (chairman), Lord Dunedin, Lord Tomlin (both law lords), Sir Shadi Lal and Sir Muhammad Sulaiman (Indian Chief Justices).

[2] For India's inchoate Commonwealth status, see p. 169, above.

[3] Report, Cmd. 4473, p. 12.   [4] Above, pp. 585–6.

[5] For an exhaustive examination of the early Commonwealth conventions, see a forthcoming book by K. C. Wheare on *Usage and Convention in the British Commonwealth*, which the writer has had the privilege of consulting in manuscript.

colonial (later called imperial) conferences had to lead to an ultimate standardization of colonial self-governing status. As soon as it was recognized that questions of status were proper to be discussed there, it was inevitable that the status of the self-governing Dominions would come to be not merely accidentally, but essentially similar, despite their unequal political development. In the War of 1914–18, a common equal status of the Dominions was a patent fact. In 1921 the Irish Treaty expressly prescribed that the new Irish Free State should have the same constitutional status as the Dominions,[1] and in 1922 its constitution provided that it should be 'a co-equal member of the Community of Nations forming the British Commonwealth of Nations'.[2] The Balfour Report of 1926 assumed throughout that each member of the Commonwealth was bound to each other member by ties that were essentially the same. Thus from being a number of isolated alleviations of the strict law, the conventions of status became a body of general doctrine. Most of the conventions of status now existing might indeed be summed up in a single rule: where laws create inequality of status, they are to be so administered by all parties as to give substantial equality in fact.

The general conventions of co-operation were under no comparable compulsion from circumstances to cohere, and they have been diversely interpreted and are not seldom disobeyed. But the coherence which they lack in execution they possess in intention. Unlike the conventions of status, they have been for the most part planned. Reports of imperial conferences repeatedly enunciate comprehensive rules for the conduct of treaty negotiations and other matters of foreign policy, and shorter sets of rules for such matters as legislation touching the succession to the Crown. All these rules are expressed in similar terms, and refer constantly to one another and to the conventions of status. Whether particular co-operative agreements are made within the context of the general conventions of co-operation or as isolated bargains is a matter which may affect the force and precision of those agreements themselves,[3] but does not affect the coherence of the general conventions.

Concerning the intimacy of the relationship between the conventions of status and the conventions of co-operation there is a differ-

---

[1] Treaty, Art. 1.   [2] Constitution, Art. 1.

[3] No contract can by its express terms cover all contingencies which may arise under it. The experience of private law shows the necessity of a background of general doctrine concerning contracts which is either incorporated into particular contracts by reference or governs them *suo proprio vigore*. International law has a similar though less well-developed doctrine concerning treaties. Commonwealth agreements are not exempt from these necessities.

ence of view between the United Kingdom and the more radical Dominions which is none the less marked because it is seldom clearly expressed. The radical Dominions naturally exalt the conventions of status, which are their title-deeds to nationhood; the United Kingdom clings to the conventions of co-operation, which are the surviving formal embodiment of imperial unity. If the government of the United Kingdom can succeed in linking the co-operative conventions intimately with the conventions of status, the Dominions may accord to the former something of the inviolability which, they insist, attaches to the latter. Documents of United Kingdom origin are thus apt to stress the mutual coherence, almost the interdependence, of conventions of status and conventions of co-operation. The classical example is the leading section of the Balfour Report[1]— a document bearing all the marks of United Kingdom authorship[2]— in which each paragraph, each sentence, almost each word imputing emancipation is balanced immediately by an assertion of association. An observer unacquainted with other terrestrial institutions might well assume, upon reading the Report, that national status and the Commonwealth association were in some sense inevitable correlatives. The radical Dominions on the other hand, who have come, perhaps a little unhistorically, to assert that they enjoy national status as of natural right, regard the conventions establishing it as tardy recognitions of eternal facts, and do not think of their emancipation as in any way qualified, still less conditioned, by the vague co-operative undertakings which of their grace they have given to their fellow-nations in the Commonwealth.

Thus the conventions of the Commonwealth are not a congeries of unrelated imperatives lacking entirely a common measure or a common design. Each of the two great classes of them shows a tendency towards that formal coherence which is one of the marks of a system of law.[3] Whether there is real coherence between the two classes themselves is more doubtful. But further speculation on this point must be postponed until after the consideration of the relation of the conventions of each class to the flanking and overshadowing systems of municipal and international law.

The present strict separation of international law from municipal systems of law dates only from the Renaissance and the Reformation,

---

[1] Cmd. 2768, pp. 14–15.

[2] It is not suggested that the United Kingdom imposed anything in the substance of the report upon the Dominions. But it is generally accepted that the drafting of the crucial parts owes more to Lord Balfour's hand than to any other.

[3] Above, p. 522.

when the sovereign state was first exalted above all other human collectivities. There is nothing in the nature of the world or of men which demands that the particular human grouping called the nation-state should be preferred above all others as it has been by the conventional morality and the law of the last three centuries. The nation did not claim primary loyalty in the Middle Ages, and the absolute claims of the Roman Empire rested not on its character as a nation among other nations, but on the false assumption that it was coterminous with civilization as a whole coupled with the truth that it was coterminous with a particular civilization and with a particular economic system. There is therefore no reason for assuming that the nation-state will for all future time be the most formally potent grouping of men. While now in some quarters nationalism is being further inflated, so that from being the prevailing it shall become the only loyalty of citizens, there are other quarters where it is losing its power. If the supremacy of the nation-state should break down in fact, its breakdown in law will doubtless follow at the usual respectful interval.

But for the present, in every civilized jurisdiction in the world municipal law prevails over all other kinds of law. Any duties the state as such may owe can only be owed to other states, and the law of states between themselves forms no part of their respective municipal laws, nor has it access to the sanctions of municipal law. Municipal law, the only law which touches and effectively governs the actions of men, is not allowed to look beyond the state and its acts except by its special grace, and, conversely, the law which alone purports to have world order as its goal may not touch a citizen of the world except by grace of his government, even though that government itself is the principal transgressor against the peace.[1] So municipal law may compel a citizen to commit an international crime, and the observance of international law or even the acknowledgment of an international loyalty may be an offence in municipal law. In a world where international contacts are by no means limited to meetings of sovereigns on fields of cloth of gold, this unnatural barrier between the instruments of international and national order is a major symptom of our present ills, and in so far as those ills are attributable to defects in institutions as distinct from policies, it is a major cause of them.[2]

---

[1] Above, p. 511. The existence of an international obligation binding Canada to legislate in a certain way does not even enlarge the power of the Dominion parliament to enable it to implement the obligation: *in re Weekly Rest in Industrial Undertakings Act &c.*, [1937] W.N. 53. But otherwise in Australia: *R.* v. *Burgess, ex. p. Henry* (1936) 10 Aust. Law Journ. 335.

[2] See, for an analysis of the fallacies which surround the idea of state sovereignty

The analogous barrier in British Commonwealth law and convention between domestic rules and the rules of the Commonwealth
association is not nearly so absolute and impenetrable. This is not
due to exceptional wisdom in Commonwealth as compared with
international statesmen, but follows inevitably from the long uncer-
tainty whether the true nation, the proper object of unique allegiance,
was each separate member of the Commonwealth or the British
Empire as a whole, and the persistence, after the matter had been
settled substantially in favour of the former, of extensive formal and
sentimental vestiges in the contrary sense.[1] But some of the consequences of the present anomalous transitional situation are none the
less fortunate for being in this sense fortuitous. In particular, it avoids
one of the most barbarous of the logical consequences of the hyper-
trophy of the sovereign state: the ticketing of all mankind with five
or six dozen sorts of labels called nationalities, each sort imposing
upon its wearers the moral and social absurdity of a unique allegiance.
The common status of British subject, though not securely anchored
in imperial fundamental law,[2] remains potent in existing municipal
law, and secures, at least to those of its possessors whose skins are
white, a large measure of equal treatment over a quarter of the sur-
face of the earth. Although for various purposes local statuses have
been created, they are not yet, even in the intention of their authors
(except in the Irish Free State),[3] mutually exclusive. This and similar
humane rules in the purely political sphere have suggested to many
of the liberal philosophers of the Empire the hope that the Commonwealth relationship may be a precursor and model for a new and saner
system of international order.

The counterpart of this hope in the juristic sphere would be the
hope that Commonwealth convention should succeed in integrating
the domestic laws of the nations of the Commonwealth with the rules
of their mutual relations into a single articulated system, in which the
loyalties claimed from the citizen by local, regional, and oecumenical
institutions should be better proportioned in their strength and
extent to the necessary and proper functions of those institutions

in international law, J. L. Brierly in *British Year Book of International Law*, 1924,
pp. 12 sqq.

[1] The chief of these, the *inter se* doctrine, described below, pp. 602–7, is a good
deal more than a vestige.

[2] Above, pp. 594–5.

[3] Though the Irish Nationality and Citizenship Act, 1935, purports to make Irish
nationality exclusive of other national statuses, the other parts of the Commonwealth
still treat the vast majority of Irish nationals as British subjects, and the citizens of
other parts of the Commonwealth in the Free State are exempted from many of the
consequences of alienage by executive order. Cf. above, p. 593.

than are the national and international allegiances now imposed upon the citizen. Though this would be a most admirable achievement, there is little to indicate that Commonwealth law and convention can attain it. Key concepts of the older systems, such as sovereignty and nationality, have filtered through to popular consciousness, and, albeit in a distorted form, command the loyalties and thereby influence the actions of men. Commonwealth law and convention have produced no concept which has comparable power over men's minds.[1]

This optimism is, perhaps a little paradoxically, one of the supports of what is called the *inter se* doctrine in the Commonwealth—a doctrine whose essence is that relations between members of the Commonwealth are *sui generis* and more intimate than relations between other nations, and that for the preservation of this uniqueness and intimacy they should be separated from international relations. Since, in the liberal optimist view, Commonwealth relations are superior in quality to international relations, and are destined to supersede them, they must be kept uncontaminated by contact with international affairs while the latter remain unregenerate. This feeling, which might be called the Liberal root of the *inter se* doctrine, overlaps and insensibly merges into its stronger Tory root, which is the sentiment that British institutions are in the nature of things superior to foreign institutions, and therefore not to be mixed with them. The *inter se* doctrine, however arrived at, may take one or other of two opposite forms. It may demand that advantage be taken of the good will between Commonwealth nations to clarify and elaborate rules to cover every contingency in the Commonwealth which is capable of regulation by law, and the institution of a Commonwealth tribunal to interpret and apply those rules; or it may hold that rules are not necessary where good will exists, and look forward to Commonwealth relations becoming like those of a family, or of the Communist classless state when law has withered away. The *inter se* doctrine in one or other of these senses, or in an intermediate form, is dominant in the United Kingdom, Australia and New Zealand, and strong in Canada. On the other hand 'radicals' in Ireland, South Africa and Canada feel that their national independence against the encroachments of Great Britain or a co-operative Commonwealth conspiracy[2] must not lack whatever prestige or protection the recognition of their full and perfect sovereignty in international law can bring. Of these two benefits, prestige must be uppermost in their minds, else the quest would be pointless at a

---

[1] Imperial symbols (Crown, flag, &c.) are not essentially *Commonwealth* ideas.

[2] Those Dominion nationalists who hold the theory of the 'Liberal Conspiracy' think advocacy of co-operation merely camouflages British 'imperialism'.

time like the present, when the security given by international law is almost negligible.

The *inter se* doctrine manifests itself in every department of Commonwealth affairs, cultural, political, legal, and conventional. It resorts to expedients of various types: where Commonwealth and international institutions differ in substance, the difference is stressed; where they do not differ in substance, they are made to differ in form; and where they do not differ even in form they are made to differ in name. Its manifestations include trivial matters of preced-ence and nomenclature, such as the practice whereby the mutual envoys of members are called not Ambassadors but High Commissioners, matters of some importance, such as the refusal to allow foreigners to participate in the settlement of Commonwealth disputes, and matters of supreme importance, such as the symbolism attached to the Crown and the fact of common citizenship. It is indeed the *differentia* of the Commonwealth among international associations.[1]

The *inter se* doctrine is perverted in many ways, notably by those who meet arguments for international co-operation either with the plea that imperial co-operation on the same lines must come first,[2] or with the plea that, since institutions or obligations of the kind proposed are not found necessary within the Empire, they are not necessary outside it.[3] Even in British official and orthodox imperialist pronouncements it often serves—in effect, if not in intention—no other purpose than that of endowing statements which are in fact controversial with a spuriously axiomatic appearance and a gratuitous emotive force. The classical expression of the application of the doctrine to the question of the international character of intra-Commonwealth relations, which is our present concern, is an example of this perversion. Sir Cecil Hurst states it thus:[4]

'If I may put the matter in one short sentence, I would say that the common allegiance to the Crown prevents the relations between the different communities being international relations.'

The word 'allegiance', though heavy with emotional content, has

---

[1] The Little Entente, for example, is knit closer by geography and by strategic common interest, and the mutual obligations of its members go in many respects beyond those of the Commonwealth; but the lack of an *inter se* doctrine places it in a different and looser class.

[2] This is the perversion suggested by the phrase 'Empire Free Trade'.

[3] This perversion is commonly used by apologists for the reluctance of Great Britain to enter into definite obligations to play her part in restraining breaches of the peace in Europe.

[4] In Lowell and Hall (ed.), *The British Commonwealth of Nations* (1927), pp. 54–5.

no meaning in law except in the particular consequences which the law ascribes to the status which it creates. Those consequences had even in 1927, when Sir Cecil Hurst wrote, not prevented the Dominions from entering into direct relations with foreign powers which were inconsistent in the sense that as a result thereof contradictory duties might be laid upon the citizens of different Dominions. If the Dominions have international personality for those purposes, it seems difficult to assert that they are *incapable* of having it for the purpose of contracting with one another. Sir Cecil Hurst's statement, then, by attributing the non-international character of Commonwealth relations to common allegiance does not explain it; it merely attaches to it the emotional reaction which is evoked by that word.[1]

In the inconclusive and intermittent controversy on this question which has gone on since the Peace, successive British governments have wavered between the view that Commonwealth relations are incapable of the character of international relations and the view that they are capable of that character, but it is undesirable that they should have it. At the other extreme, Irish governments have asserted the completely and exclusively international character of the Free State's relations with other members of the Commonwealth; with this *nuance*, that the Cumann na nGaedheal Government was at pains to assert the validity of the Treaty of 1922 in international law, while the Fianna Fáil Government has taken the line that it is either invalid upon the ground of duress or so unconscionable that its binding force is thereby impaired. South African governments, at least since General Hertzog took office in 1924, have consistently held that South Africa's relations with other Commonwealth nations are potentially international, but that South Africa applies the *inter se* doctrine of her own free will. Liberal, but not Conservative, governments in Canada have taken a similar line.

The basic question whether the Covenant of the League of Nations could be invoked by a member of the Commonwealth in a dispute with another member has never been decided.[2] But it is the separate membership of the Dominions in the League of Nations that has been the chief ground of most subsequent assertions of the separate international personality of the Dominions both in substance and in law.

---

[1] See, for another criticism of this dictum, P. J. Noel Baker, *The Present Juridical Status of the British Dominions in International Law* (1929), pp. 298 sqq. Sir Stafford Cripps expressed the same verbalistic outlook when he said of the Irish Treaty: 'It is an agreement. It is impossible in law for one sovereign to enter into a treaty with himself.' (259 *H. C. Deb.*, 5s., 695, 17th June 1932.)

[2] For an exhaustive and able discussion of this question, see P. J. Noel Baker, op. cit., pp. 305–18.

The first formal dispute was that concerning the registration of the Anglo-Irish Treaty of 1921 with the Secretariat of the League under Article 18 of the Covenant.[1] In 1924 the Free State Government presented the Treaty for registration, and the Secretary-General of the League, whose functions under the Article are automatic, registered it. The British Government wrote to the Secretary-General that:

'Since the Covenant of the League of Nations came into force, His Majesty's Government have consistently taken the view that neither it, nor any conventions concluded under the auspices of the League, are intended to govern the relations *inter se* of the various parts of the British Commonwealth. His Majesty's Government consider, therefore, that the terms of Article 18 of the Covenant are not applicable to the Articles of Agreement of 6th December, 1921.'[2]

The Free State Government replied:

'The obligations contained in Article 18 are, in their opinion, imposed in the most specific terms on every member of the League and they are unable to accept the contention that the clear and unequivocal language of that Article is susceptible of any interpretation compatible with the limitation which the British Government now seek to read into it.'[3]

The controversy went no farther.

In 1926 the Imperial Conference made the following declaration:[4]

'The making of [a] treaty in the name of the King as the symbol of the special relationship between the different parts of the Empire will render superfluous the inclusion of any provision that its terms must not be regarded as regulating *inter se* the rights and obligations of the various territories on behalf of which it has been signed by the King. In this connexion it must be borne in mind that the question was discussed at the Arms Traffic Conference in 1925, and that the Legal Committee of that Conference laid it down that the principle to which the foregoing sentence gives expression underlies all international conventions.

'In the case of some international agreements the Governments of different parts of the Empire may be willing to apply between themselves some of the provisions as an administrative measure. In this case they should state the extent to which and the terms on which such provisions are to apply. Where international agreements are to be

---

[1] Article 18 reads: 'Every treaty or international engagement entered into hereafter by any member of the League shall be forthwith registered with the Secretariat and shall as soon as possible be published by it. No such treaty or international engagement shall be binding until so registered.'
[2] League of Nations, *Treaty Series*, xxvii. Printed in the *Survey of International Affairs for 1924*, p. 474. See pp. 150, 321, above.
[3] Loc. cit.   [4] Cmd. 2768, p. 23.

applied between different parts of the Empire, the form of a treaty between Heads of States should be avoided.'

These words form part of a set of rules, which are perhaps hardly more than recommendations,[1] for the making of treaties by the members of the Commonwealth, and touch our problem only obliquely. They were undoubtedly drawn up with the Irish Treaty question in mind. Being an agreed text, they cannot even be construed as amounting to an abandonment by Great Britain of the view that international treaties are *incapable* of applying to members of the Commonwealth *inter se*, though upon a strict construction this might be inferred from the admission that either an express contrary provision or signature in the name of the King is required to prevent a treaty from so applying. It is suggested rather than laid down that it is not desirable that future treaties should be made to apply *suo proprio vigore*, by virtue of international law, between members of the Commonwealth. Nothing is said of the Irish Treaty, or of the eligibility of intra-Commonwealth agreements in general for registration under Article 18 of the Covenant.[2] The question whether imperial relations shall be international relations is left open, with a suggestion that they should not normally be given an international character. It now becomes clear, however, that the issue will be determined by practice and, possibly, agreement, not by dogma.

The attitude of the governments of the Commonwealth to the submission of Commonwealth disputes to the Permanent Court of International Justice exhibits with unusual clarity the way in which the *inter se* doctrine is regarded in the various Dominions.[3] In 1929 Great Britain and all the Dominions adhered for the first time to the 'Optional Clause' of the Statute of the Court. States so adhering recognize the jurisdiction of the Court as 'compulsory, *ipso facto* and without special agreement' in relation to all other States adhering to the Clause in practically all disputes of a legal character. The Court is not an arbitral body or tribunal in equity, but a tribunal of strict international law. To admit the competence of the Court in a dispute is, therefore, to admit that the dispute is one of international law.

[1] The part quoted cannot be taken as laying down hard-and-fast rules, for its principal recommendation, namely, that treaties should be made in the names of Heads of States, requires the concurrence of the foreign parties.

[2] The view taken by Mr. Noel Baker in his extended treatment of the matter (op. cit., pp. 289–301), that the Conference resolution amounts to a defeat for the Irish view, seems therefore to go too far.

[3] See, for a fuller account of the adhesions of 1929, Sir John Fischer Williams in *British Year Book of International Law*, 1930, p. 63.

The United Kingdom made its adherence subject to the reservation of—

> 'Disputes with the Government of any other member of the League which is a member of the British Commonwealth of Nations, all of which disputes shall be settled in such manner as the parties have agreed or shall agree.' [1]

Mr. Henderson, the Foreign Secretary, explained the reservation by the official theory that—

> 'the Members of the Commonwealth, though international units individually in the fullest sense of the term, are united by their common allegiance to the Crown. Disputes between them should therefore be dealt with by some other mode of settlement.' [2]

Canada, Australia, South Africa, New Zealand, and India made the same reservation. The Canadian and South African delegates made supplementary declarations to the effect that they withheld jurisdiction in Commonwealth disputes not because they considered them incapable of submission to the Permanent Court, but as a matter of policy. The Irish Free State adhered without any reservation at all.

In 1930 the Imperial Conference drew up a scheme for voluntary *ad hoc* tribunals in justiciable inter-Imperial disputes.[3] Nothing was said of the law to be applied by these bodies, but the *inter se* principle appeared in the shape of a provision that the personnel of tribunals should be drawn entirely from within the Commonwealth. There is, of course, nothing to prevent Commonwealth judges applying international law. In the controversy between the Irish Free State and the United Kingdom over the Land Annuities in 1932, the Free State government refused to accept the restriction of the membership of a proposed arbitral body to the Commonwealth. This demand, conversely, does not strictly amount to an assertion that Commonwealth relations are governed by international law. There is, however, no doubt that Mr. de Valera's government holds even more emphatically than did its predecessor that they are.

While no progress has been made towards the ultimate decision whether or not the rules of the Commonwealth will come within the fold of general international law or remain a separate system, Commonwealth law and convention have undergone several changes

---

[1] Cmd. 3452, p. 5; *Documents on International Affairs*, 1929, p. 39.
[2] Cmd. 3452, p. 6; ibid., p. 42. Cf. Hurst, above, p. 603.
[3] Cmd. 3717, pp. 22–4.

which bring them nearer in character to international law, and farther from municipal law. Most of these have already been referred to in other connexions. The assertion of local roots for the law of certain Dominions[1] endows them with formally separate systems of municipal law, and therefore separate individualities in ultimate constitutional theory, parallel to the separate personalities which all the Dominions have for some time enjoyed in international law. For the Dominions which have not asserted local roots for their laws, the growth of the distinction between imperial and local fundamental law[2] has performed a similar service in a milder way, accentuating the distinctness of their constitutional individualities without severing them entirely from the United Kingdom and each other in their ultimate constitutional theory. More important than either of these developments in strict law is the tendency towards clearer demarcation between the conventions of status, which supplement municipal law, and the conventions of co-operation, whose function is in all respects analogous to that of international law.[3]

A small but significant phenomenon is the endowment of the members of the Commonwealth as such with rudimentary corporate personalities (which must be distinguished from the constitutional individualities above referred to)[4] in strict imperial constitutional law. It has long been a convention of Commonwealth relations, as of international affairs, that a nation expresses its will only through its executive government. Suggestions that leaders of Oppositions as well as Prime Ministers might attend Imperial Conferences have been repeatedly rejected on this ground. But not until very recently have 'Canada', 'Australia'—or even 'the United Kingdom'—appeared as dramatis personae as distinct from mere properties on the stage of strict law. These names have long been used in statutes in adjectival phrases descriptive of institutions corporate and incorporate, and alone as geographical substantives, but never by themselves to designate national entities deemed to have single corporate wills of their own. 'Great Britain' and 'Ireland', persons hitherto unknown to the law, appeared as the parties to the 'Articles of Agreement for a Treaty' which were scheduled to the Irish Free State (Agreement) Act 1922. These mysterious and commanding figures presided, like premature Magi, over the birth of the Free

---

[1] Above, Section II (1).   [2] Above, pp. 577, 582.   [3] Above, pp. 597–9.

[4] Personality in the strict legal sense means the quality of being the subject of legal rights and duties. It is possessed by natural persons (human beings) and by 'bodies corporate', but not by 'unincorporated' collectivities or organisms. The law is said to 'incorporate' an entity when it makes it capable of rights and duties. 'Individuality' is here used descriptively, without any technical meaning.

State, and have not appeared again. Heads still ache all over the Commonwealth, and skulls are still cracked in Ireland, over the question of their identity and the significance of their brief act. (But these matters are less urgent now, for the spells they wove have almost ceased to bind.) Section 2 of the Statute of Westminster provides that no future statute of the Imperial Parliament shall apply to a Dominion as part of the law of that Dominion unless the request and consent *of that Dominion* are declared in the preamble. Who is this person, the Dominion, who has a tongue to request and a mind to consent ? When the Statute was drafted the Australian representatives, affecting a proper judicial ignorance, complained of the imprecision of the reference. But the other Dominions were not to be cheated of the scintilla of personal status which the section implied, and in a supplementary section[1] the phrase was defined for Australia, but for no other Dominion, as meaning the request and consent of the Parliament of the Dominion. In His Majesty's Declaration of Abdication Act, 1936, the 'request and consent' recited was that of 'Canada' *simpliciter*, and the 'assents' recited were likewise those of 'Australia', 'South Africa', and 'New Zealand'. In fact, the expressions of approval of the Act to which the recital referred all emanated from the governments concerned and not from the parliaments, with the single exception, again, of Australia.[2] Thus the new legal persons performed their first act in law. We may expect that in future imperial statutes applying to the Dominions—if there are any—the veil will be drawn more thickly over the internal organization of the Dominions, and the single will of the Dominion government will wherever possible be left to speak alone, in the name of the Dominion as a legal person, to the outside world, equally within or without the Commonwealth. The assimilation to international practice is clear.

In sum, it appears that the law and convention of the Commonwealth is likely to disappoint those who hoped it would bring a positive contribution to the framing of a new and better rule of international order. As its doctrine becomes more definite its shape follows more and more exactly the familiar outlines of international law, despite its remaining for the present, in the view of most members of the Commonwealth, a formally separate system. This

[1] s. 9 (1).

[2] The resolution of the Australian Parliament on 11th December 1936 was not designed to satisfy s. 9 (1), for the Statute of Westminster does not yet apply to Australia, and the Abdication Act came into effect there *suo proprio vigore*. It was designed to satisfy the convention concerning laws regarding the succession agreed upon in 1929 and 1930 and recited in the preamble to the Statute.

does not mean that certain of its negative aspects may not fulfil a modest but not negligible fraction of liberal hopes. Its greatest achievement in this direction has been in the matter of common citizenship. Experience has shown that within an association such as the Commonwealth, in which the contingency of war between the members need not be provided for, the fullest measure of national self-government under the traditional form of the sovereign state does not necessitate the confining of civic and political rights in the several nations to persons belonging to mutually exclusive national categories.[1] National sovereignty is compatible with common or reciprocal citizenship within any group of nations which does not contemplate internecine war. The demonstration of the possibility of such a common citizenship arrangement is a real contribution to the technique of a world order.

It remains to consider the relation of Commonwealth conventions to municipal law. The very definition of constitutional convention is a negative one: it consists of those usages of public men and public bodies which are thought of as obligatory for some other reason than that they are cognizable in a court of law. A convention may be thought obligatory for that reason as well, that is to say, a law may coincide with it; but in such cases the convention is normally super-fluous because of the superior authority and efficacy of law. Only where the force of law is for some reason attenuated is it worth while inquiring whether a rule of convention exists parallel to the rule of law.

A convention may be derived from custom or from agreement. In domestic affairs agreement rarely, if ever, creates constitutional convention, because the usual parties—namely ministers, members of Parliament, the Houses of Parliament, and the King—have not moral authority to bind their successors by mere agreement apart from precedent. But in Commonwealth relations it has long been recognized that the agreement of the executive government of a member binds its successors, because it would be derogatory to its autonomy if other members, in order to ascertain their rights and obligations in relation to it, were compelled to examine its internal affairs. Agreed conventions are accordingly common in Common-

[1] The Irish Free State, which is the only member of the Commonwealth which seeks to make its citizenship exclusive of other Commonwealth citizenships—and even that with such palliatives as to make the British or Dominion visitor in effect much more nearly a citizen than an alien—is the exception which proves the rule, for it is the only Dominion where there is not an overwhelming conviction that war with another member of the Commonwealth is unthinkable.

wealth affairs, the chief of them being the conventions agreed upon at Imperial Conferences. A certain difficulty arises over those conventions of status to which the parties are a Dominion or Dominions on the one side and some organ in the United Kingdom constitution other than the executive government, such as the Imperial Parliament, on the other. It is very doubtful whether Parliament would be prepared to assent to the proposition that the United Kingdom government of the day has general authority to commit even the existing parliament, let alone its successors, to whatever conventional obligations ministers may concert with Dominion governments.[1] At least, one can easily imagine circumstances in which a succeeding, or even the same parliament, might revolt against such obligations.[2] So far as the current parliament at least is concerned, the recital of such conventions in a preamble to a statute may be thought to mend matters somewhat, by expressing Parliament's consent.[3] The difficulty is less where the convention is negative, binding Parliament *not* to act, than where it imposes a positive obligation to legislate to a certain effect: Parliament is less likely to jib at being told not to legislate[4] than at being told that it

[1] Professor J. L. Brierly has drawn the attention of the writer to the circumstances in which the Empire Marketing Board was established. Mr. Baldwin at the Imperial Conference of 1923 promised the Dominions certain preferential duties. He was put out of office before he could implement this promise, and regained office in the next year on a pledge not to impose a tariff. He and his majority, however, felt so far bound by the pledge that a sum equivalent to the amount of the intended remission of duties to the Dominions was voted for the establishment of the Empire Marketing Board. Any obligation there may have been in this case was, of course, not a general convention of status, but an isolated co-operative convention. In such matters it is probable that Commonwealth arrangements will be treated in the same way as international agreements, for whose coming into force Great Britain does not, but the Dominions generally do, insist on parliamentary ratification.

[2] Some hold the view (with which the writer does not agree) that the second recital in the Statute of Westminster requires the *prior* assent of all the parliaments of the Commonwealth before legislation touching the succession can be properly passed by the imperial parliament. On this view, the enactment of His Majesty's Declaration of Abdication Act, 1936, before the *Parliaments* of Canada, South Africa, New Zealand, and the Irish Free State had assented to it was a breach of convention, and furnishes an admirable instance of the difficulty of binding Parliament even by a negative contractual convention.

[3] It is difficult to assign any other force than this to such recitals, and therefore difficult to regard recital in a preamble as a third mode of creating convention, in addition to precedent and agreement, as Dr. Jennings does (*The Law and the Constitution*, p. 86). Conventions so recited would have no force unless they had been agreed upon beforehand by the governments of the Commonwealth, at an imperial conference or otherwise; and once so agreed upon, they bind the governments without recital in a statute.

[4] Since a government nowadays can always prevent legislation, it is really sufficient, to secure the observance by Parliament of negative conventions, that the government is bound by them.

has to pass automatically without amendment some text from over-seas.

There is some difficulty in distinguishing between law and conven-tion in Commonwealth affairs, because many major topics in the Commonwealth are so seldom adjudicated upon by the courts that it is a matter of speculation what rules the courts would recognize and what they would not. The task of distinguishing has not been rendered easier by the ambiguities and the conflicts of view con-cerning the formal derivation of Dominion law, or by the develop-ments described in the preceding section of this chapter. In that section we have seen how, in certain respects and for certain Do-minions, rules of imperial unity which formerly rested on law have come to be regarded as having the force of convention merely,[1] so that they are not distinguishable in effect from the conventions of co-operation.

But if Commonwealth co-operation is becoming increasingly a sphere of convention, and decreasingly of law, the equal status of the members of the Commonwealth, which was established almost entirely by the development of conventions, is steadily acquiring the quality of law. By one means and another, the conventions of status are being translated into law. A parallel transformation is taking place in the domestic sphere: the Parliament Act, 1911, and the Irish Free State Constitution[2] are instances of the substitution of law for domestic constitutional convention;[3] but there the pace is slow. In the Commonwealth there have been only a few statutes of this type, but the gap between law and fact has been so wide, and the conse-quent pressure for its reduction so great that these few statutes have been the vehicle of a change out of proportion to the modesty of their wording, at least as that wording is read by the lawyer accus-tomed to the ungenerous English tradition of statutory interpre-tation.[4]

[1] Above, p. 582.
[2] e.g. Art. 24 (Oireachtas to fix the beginning and end of its sessions); Art. 24 as amended in 1936 (Chairman of Dáil to summon and dissolve Dáil on advice of Execu-tive Council); Art. 28 (Dáil not to be dissolved except on such advice); Art. 35 (definition of money bills); Art. 41 as amended in 1936 (duty of Chairman to sign bills presented to him); Art. 51 until 1936 (see above, p. 586); Art. 51 (Executive Council to be responsible to Dáil Éireann); Art. 53 (Dáil to choose President of the Executive Council; President to choose members of Executive Council; Dáil not to be dissolved by Executive Council without a majority in Dáil); Art. 54 (collective responsibility of Executive Council).
[3] Mr. Justice Evatt's recent book, *The King and his Dominion Governors*, is a plea for the conversion of the conventions governing the relation between King (or Governor) and Parliament into law.
[4] e.g. *British Coal Corporation* v. *R.*, [1935] A.C. 500. See above, p. 557.

The first notable instance of the translation of Commonwealth convention into law is to be seen in the Irish Treaty, which provided[1] that

> 'Subject to the provisions hereinafter set out the position of the Irish Free State in relation to the Imperial Parliament and Government and otherwise shall be that of the Dominion of Canada, and the law, practice and constitutional usage governing the relationship of the Crown or of the Representative of the Crown and of the Imperial Parliament to the Dominion of Canada shall govern their relationship to the Irish Free State.'

By the Constitution of the Irish Free State (Saorstát Éireann) Act[2] and the Irish Free State Constitution Act, 1922,[3] this provision was 'given the force of law'. Thus the 'practice and constitutional usage' referred to was not merely applied in its original character to the new Dominion but given the character of law there.[4] This situation was remarkable in that the existence of the conventions which were to become law was left to be determined by the courts which might have occasion to apply the law.[5]

Other statutes have enacted as law rules which cover ground which was previously covered by convention. The chief of these are the Statute of Westminster, 1931,[6] the Status of the Union Act, 1934,[7] and Royal Executive Functions and Seals Act, 1934,[8] of South Africa, and the Constitution (Amendment No. 27) Act, 1936,[9] and Executive Authority (External Relations) Act, 1936,[10] of the Irish Free State. The effect of these statutes cannot be summarized here, but they have converted a considerable proportion of the conventions of status, in their application to Canada, South Africa, and the Irish Free State, into law.

It has been suggested that the opinion read by Lord Sankey for the Judicial Committee in *British Coal Corporation* v. *R.*[11] opens up the prospect that the Courts may take it upon themselves to recog-

---

[1] Art. 2.   [2] No. 1 of 1922 of the Constituent Assembly, s. 2.

[3] 13 Geo. 5, c. 1, s. 1.

[4] S. 2 of the Constituent Act has been repealed by the Constitution (Removal of Oath) Act, No. 6 of 1933. Whether this repeal undoes the incorporation of convention into law referred to in the text is doubtful.

[5] But in fact, by reason of the reluctance of bench, bar, and litigants to emphasize the Dominion status as against the national status of the Free State, this section and the corresponding provision of s. 51 until its amendment in 1926 have seldom been invoked in Free State courts. It was cited in vain before the Judicial Committee in *Performing Right Society* v. *Bray U.D.C.*, [1930] A.C. 377, 383.

[6] 22 Geo. 5, c. 4.   [7] No. 69 of 1934. Above, pp. 531. Below, p. 617.

[8] No. 70 of 1934. Above, p. 590.   [9] No. 57 of 1936. Above, p. 586, n. 2.

[10] No. 58 of 1936. Above, p. 586, n. 2.   [11] [1935] A.C. 500.

nize judicially certain well-established conventions, thereby giving them the force of law. In the view of Dr. Jennings,[1] the Board in this case confessedly took into account two conventions in arriving at the conclusion that, apart from external fetters, the power of the Canadian parliament under the British North America Act, 1867, includes the power to abolish the jurisdiction of the Judicial Committee in criminal appeals from Canada—the convention that the Judicial Committee, though legally part of an executive body, is a court of law, and the convention that, though in law it belongs to the executive of the United Kingdom, it is really a Canadian, or at least not merely a United Kingdom court. The words of the opinion certainly lend colour to this view; but it would take more than a single decision of the Judicial Committee to establish such a radical innovation in the law. It is perhaps best to treat the case as an extreme instance of the liberal or 'living tree' interpretation of the Canadian Constitution, and one which is by no means certain to be followed in later cases. Such confusion, from the lawyer's point of view, would result from a breakdown of the barrier between law and convention that it can hardly be anticipated that the courts will allow it to occur. But the case does serve to show how thin that barrier has become.

It seems accordingly to be the destiny of the conventions of Commonwealth status to be gradually incorporated into strict municipal law, possibly with the aid of judicial decision but principally by the instrumentality of imperial and Dominion statutes. This means that the *corpus* of Commonwealth convention will come to consist preponderantly, if not entirely, of the conventions of co-operation. They, and not the decreasing residue of conventions of status, will determine the general character of Commonwealth convention. Except on one point, generalizations concerning their future can be no more than speculation. But it seems certain that, whatever the formal relation of Commonwealth convention to the system of international law may come to be, the substance of its rules and concepts is likely, for want of intrinsic fertility or an alternative model, to approximate more and more closely to the analogy of international law. Any superiority which its rules may have over those of international law will be a negative one, arising from the refusal of the members of the Commonwealth to apply in their mutual relations the more extreme perversities of excessive nationalism. Now, as in the seventeenth century, the rules of the British Empire, whether

[1] 52 *L.Q.R.* 177–9.

they are called law or convention, will follow the facts. It has never been the British habit that they should do otherwise. All that can fairly be demanded of them is that, in a time when the very essence of the institutions to which they are attached is rapidly changing, they too should accelerate their rate of change, so as not to lag too far behind.

If Commonwealth convention joins the system of international law, it will cease to have a separate doctrinal history. If it stays separate, the alternatives of greater precision and vague equity, whose ideals are the 'Commonwealth tribunal' and the 'happy family' respectively, will remain. Prediction is difficult, but at present it seems probable that precision will prevail. There can be no real precision in any body of rules without a permanent tribunal having a general jurisdiction to interpret and apply them in a strictly judicial manner. The *ad hoc* tribunals of the 1930 Conference would be nearly useless for this purpose, even if the necessity for preliminary agreement on their personnel and terms of reference did not render them unattainable in a dispute of any acerbity. But before an effective tribunal having jurisdiction in Commonwealth convention can be set up, the relation of Commonwealth convention to international and municipal law must be settled by agreement. To many it is a matter of surprise and regret that the members of the Commonwealth, who were ready in 1929 to accord a large measure of compulsory jurisdiction to a predominantly foreign court in disputes with foreign nations, have not been able to reach a similarly reasonable arrangement among themselves. But in committing these disputes to the Hague Court, to be judged by international law, they had some idea of what they were committing themselves to. If at the present moment the members of the Commonwealth were to set up a court with the same power which the Hague Court in effect enjoys to 'find its own law', there is no knowing what its judges, set to find their way through the maze of Commonwealth rules by the light of reason alone, might not decide.

APPENDIX

THE ABDICATION OF KING EDWARD VIII IN COMMONWEALTH LAW AND CONVENTION

THE RELEVANT RULES OF LAW

I. The abdication of a monarch and the installation of a successor, whether or not the successor installed is the next in natural succession to the Throne, cannot take effect in the law of the United Kingdom or of any of the Dominions by act of the monarch, or otherwise except by statute.

> This seems the best view. There is no true precedent of a voluntary abdication.[1] But the rule as stated seems to follow inevitably from the fact that the title to the Throne is parliamentary. The law officers in the United Kingdom and in all the Dominions except South Africa concurred in this view. The writer, with respect, agrees.
>
> The view of the advisers of the South African government, which was accepted by that government,[2] is that a monarch may abdicate by his own act,[3] but, *semble*, that such abdication does not of itself disinherit his unborn issue, if any.[4]

II. (*a*) In United Kingdom law,[5] a statute of the United Kingdom parliament for the removal of a monarch and the installation of a successor validly effects that change for the United Kingdom, Australia, New Zealand, Newfoundland, and their dependencies independently of any recitals in its preamble.

(*b*) In United Kingdom law, *semble*, such a statute likewise effects that change for the Union of South Africa and its dependencies.

(*c*) *Quaere*, whether in United Kingdom law such a statute takes effect for Canada or the Irish Free State unless the request and consent of Canada or the Irish Free State, as the case may be, is recited in its preamble.

[1] For a clear exposition of the precedents, see the speech of Mr. Menzies in the Australian House of Representatives, 12th December 1936.

[2] The terms of the proclamation of the accession of King George VI in the Union on 12th December are the first evidence of the adoption of this view. On 11th December General Hertzog addressed a telegram to his predecessor as King, although on this view of the law he had ceased to be King on 10th December. General Hertzog later explained in the House of Assembly on 25th January 1937 that this style was used for reasons of courtesy.

[3] Mr. R. B. Bennett appeared to give his adherence to this view in the Canadian House of Commons on 18th January.

[4] This factor, Mr. Pirow explained in the House of Assembly on 27th January, was what necessitated legislation by the South African Parliament. His view is reflected in the wording of His Majesty King Edward VIII's Abdication Bill, 1937, cl. 2.

[5] i.e. in the law applied by the courts of the United Kingdom of Great Britain and Northern Ireland and its dependencies.

(*d*) *Et quaere*, whether in United Kingdom law, in the absence of a United Kingdom statute containing such a recital, a statute of the Oireachtas or of the Canadian parliament, as the case may be, can validly effect the change for its Dominion.

(*a*) Since the Statute of Westminster does not apply to Australia, New Zealand, and Newfoundland, the United Kingdom statute applies there of its own force as an imperial statute extending thereto by 'express words or necessary intendment' within the meaning of the Colonial Laws Validity Act, 1865, s. 1.

(*b*) The Statute of Westminster does apply to the Union of South Africa, but its operation in this particular matter is, in the opinion of the writer, circumvented by ss. 2 (as amended by s. 5 of the Status of the Union Act, 1934) and 3 of the South Africa Act, 1909. These sections, taken together, have provided since 1934 that the King for the purposes of the South Africa Act shall include 'His Majesty's heirs in the sovereignty of the United Kingdom of Great Britain and Ireland[1] as determined by the laws relating to the succession of the Crown of the United Kingdom of Great Britain and Ireland'. There is no doubt that the amendment in this sense of the South Africa Act by the Status of the Union Act is valid, whatever may be thought of the validity of other sections of the Status of the Union Act.[2] Nor is there, in the opinion of the writer, any doubt that, by reason of its greater particularity, s. 5 of the Status of the Union Act prevails over the provision of s. 2 of the same Act that no statute of the United Kingdom parliament shall apply to the Union unless adopted by the Union Parliament,[3] whatever the validity of that provision may be.[2] But it may be doubted whether the laws of the United Kingdom thus adopted include statutes passed after the date of the Status of the Union Act itself, such as His Majesty's Declaration of Abdication Act, 1936. In view of the provision of the latter Act for a demise of the Crown, there is little doubt that in this particular instance King George VI took the Throne as 'heir'. The South African government, however, did not regard the Act as applying to the Union.[4]

(*c*) Section 4 of the Statute of Westminster provides that 'No Act of Parliament of the United Kingdom passed after the commencement of this Act shall extend, or be deemed to extend, to a Dominion as part of the law of that Dominion, unless it is expressly declared in that Act that that Dominion has requested, and consented to, the enactment thereof.' The predominant view among United Kingdom jurists is that the inalienable sovereignty of the United Kingdom parliament enables it validly to pass an Act disregarding the limitation which this section purports to impose. On this view the section has no effect in law beyond raising a presumption, in cases of ambiguity whether or not an Act is intended to apply to the Dominions, that it does not apply if the requirements of the

---

[1] *Sic.* The Status of the Union Act throughout erroneously refers to 'the United Kingdom of Great Britain and Ireland' instead of 'the United Kingdom of Great Britain and Northern Ireland'.   [2] See above, pp. 532–4.

[3] But Mr. John Foster is not certain on this point. See *The Nineteenth Century*, February 1937, p. 234.

[4] General Hertzog in the House of Assembly, 25th January.

section have not been complied with. Others hold that the section is valid until repealed expressly or by implication by an Act which itself recites the request and consent of the Dominions in respect of which it is desired to repeal the section. The section applies without qualification to Canada and the Irish Free State.

(d) The British North America Act and the various constituent documents of the Irish Free State do not, in the view of United Kingdom law, themselves grant to their respective parliaments power to pass legislation affecting the succession to the Throne. It is a matter of doubt whether, in United Kingdom law, the additional power conferred by s. 2 of the Statute of Westminster extends to authorize such legislation.[1]

III. The laws of Canada, Australia, New Zealand, and Newfoundland concur with the law of the United Kingdom in the above rules.

The legal systems of Canada, Australia, New Zealand, and Newfoundland belong to the imperial system of law, and therefore cannot conflict with the law of the United Kingdom.[2]

IV. (a) *Semble*, in the law of South Africa, Rule I will no longer hold good, and a monarch may abdicate on his own behalf, but not on behalf of his unborn issue (*quaere*, as to existing issue), by his own act, both for South Africa and for the other parts of the Commonwealth.

(b) *Semble*, the law of South Africa concurs with the law of the United Kingdom in Rule II (b).

(c) In all other respects, the law of South Africa concurs with the law of the United Kingdom.

(a) See comments on Rule I. His Majesty King Edward VIII's Declaration of Abdication Bill, 1937,[3] of the Union expressly purports to establish in South African law the view taken by the government, and will probably be effective in doing so.[4]

(b) The government of the Union dissents from Rule II (b), and therefore from the rule here stated. The Bill does not touch the question. The writer, with respect, prefers the view here stated.[5]

V. Probably, in the law of the Irish Free State, an Act of the United Kingdom parliament to the above effect, whatever its recitals, true or false, does not effect the change for the Free State, and has effect in the other parts of the British Commonwealth according to their respective laws.

If this is so, an Act of the Oireachtas is competent, in the view of the law of the Irish Free State, to effect the change for the Irish Free State.

The position is complicated and obscure. In Free State law, the United Kingdom enjoys no inherent right to legislate, by any procedure, for the

---

[1] See above, pp. 588–9.   [2] See above, pp. 526–7.
[3] This Bill had not been passed at the time of going to press. The writer has assumed that it would be passed in its then form.
[4] See above, pp. 532–4.
[5] For the reasons stated in the comment to Rule II (b), above.

Free State. Any right it has so to legislate must be conferred by the Treaty. *Quaere*, whether the Treaty does purport to confer any such right. In the view of the present government of the Free State, and probably, but not certainly, in the view of the Free State courts (from which no appeal now lies to the Privy Council), the Constitution of the Free State is no longer subject to the Treaty. But *quaere* whether, if the Treaty has been effectively removed from the fundamental law of the Free State by the Constitution (Removal of Oath) Act, 1933, the provisions of the Treaty, if any, identifying the Irish with the English law of succession were not still, at the time of the passing of the United Kingdom Abdication Act, valid ordinary law of the Free State.

If in Free State law the Constitution is not now subject to the Treaty, there is no doubt of the power of the Oireachtas to pass legislation affecting the succession for the Free State. If it is so subject, it is very questionable whether, apart from the Statute of Westminster, the Oireachtas has such power. The view of the present government that the Statute cannot confer any additional power rests on its view that the Constitution is not subject to the Treaty: so *quaere* whether, if the Constitution is subject to the Treaty, the Statute may not operate to confer the necessary power.

THE RELEVANT CONVENTIONS

I. It is the constitutional duty of any parliament in the Commonwealth (or at least of the United Kingdom parliament) not to enact any alteration of the law touching the succession to the Throne or the royal style and titles unless the other parliaments of the Commonwealth have first assented thereto; but where such legislation is urgently necessary and the prior consultation of all the parliaments is impracticable within the time available, subsequent assent by the parliaments is sufficient, if before the enactment the initiating government has obtained from the other governments their assent, their promise that they will seek the assent of their parliaments, and their assurance that there is a reasonable certainty that that assent will not be withheld.

This rule results from the convention agreed upon at the Imperial Conference of 1930[1] which appears as the second recital of the Statute of Westminster, that

'inasmuch as the Crown is the symbol of the free association of the members of the British Commonwealth of Nations, and as they are united by a common allegiance to the Crown, it would be in accord with the established constitutional position of all the members of the Commonwealth in relation to one another that any alteration in the law touching the Succession to the Throne or the Royal Style and Titles shall hereafter require the assent as well of the Parliaments of all the Dominions as of the Parliament of the United Kingdom.'

The provision in an abdication statute for an artificial demise of the Crown is perhaps not technically an alteration in the law touching the succession; but the inevitable clause disinheriting the issue of the abdicating monarch is.

[1] Cmd. 3717, p. 21.

The gloss for cases of urgency is a practical necessity. Its introduction is justified by the rule, which governs the interpretation of all convention, that conventions are made to work.

II. It is the constitutional duty of any minister or government in the Commonwealth not to do anything from which a situation necessitating legislation of the above categories may result, without first consulting the other governments of the Commonwealth.

This is a corollary of Rule I, on the assumption that constitutional conventions are concerned rather with the substance than with the form of Commonwealth relations. On this view, the creation without consultation of a situation where legislation of the specified kind is inevitable is no less obnoxious to the convention than the enactment of it without consultation.

III. Independently of the two preceding rules, it is the constitutional duty of any minister or government in the Commonwealth not to tender to the monarch constitutionally significant advice in a matter of common concern, without first consulting the other governments of the Commonwealth.

IV. For the purpose of Rule III, advice is constitutionally significant whether it is tendered formally or informally, finally or tentatively, subject or not subject to reservation, if it is of such a character that in all the circumstances it is reasonably to be contemplated that the monarch may, rightly or wrongly, feel a constitutional obligation to comply with it.

V. For the purposes of Rule III, a matter is of common concern to the extent that it directly affects more than one member of the Commonwealth if in relation to that matter the monarch cannot, whether for reasons of nature, of law, or of convention, take separate action on behalf of each member concerned.

VI. For the purposes of these rules, the obligation to consult another government is satisfied if that government is accurately informed of the proposed action, and is given an opportunity to express its views to the initiating party before action is taken and, if the contemplated action is advice to the Crown, to tender advice of its own at the same time as advice is tendered by the initiating party.

VII. It is the constitutional duty of the monarch to see to the best of his ability that the conventions of Commonwealth consultation are complied with in respect of advice tendered to him, and therefore probably to disregard advice tendered in breach of them.

These rules, especially Rules III to V, are difficult to formulate, and some will disagree with the above formulation of them, especially with Rule IV. There is not space to justify them in detail here, but in the opinion of the writer they follow from three established principles: (*a*) that the members of the Commonwealth have equal status in their mutual relations in all substantial respects; (*b*) that the Crown is a common Crown, belonging to all equally; (c) that Commonwealth constitutional convention, in the absence of express provision to the contrary, is a matter of good sense and good faith, looking not to formalities, but to the substance of transactions.[1]

THE COURSE OF EVENTS

1936. 20th January.

King Edward VIII acceded to the Throne. For some time before his accession he had associated consistently with Mrs. Ernest Simpson, a lady of American birth possessing British nationality by virtue of her marriage to her second husband. Her first, an American citizen, had been divorced by her in the United States, and was at all relevant times still living.

The association continued after the King's accession. He sought neither concealment nor publicity for it.

August, September, and October.

Reports of the matter, compounded in varying degrees of fact and fiction, appeared in the American and foreign press. During this period these reports came to exceed by far the proportions of ordinary speculative gossip on such subjects both in volume and in credibility.

Practically the whole of the press of the British Empire, whether by unanimous coincidence of individual decisions (as some newspapers afterwards asserted) or by concerted action, and whether freely or with knowledge of the wide and uncertain scope of the law of seditious libel, made no open allusion to the matter and suppressed most of the reports and photographs which were evidence of it. Except in Canada, where American newspapers are imported and read in large quantities, the great bulk of public opinion in the Empire was accordingly unaware of the matter.

The Prime Minister of Canada was in the United Kingdom on a private visit from 16th October to 31st October. During this visit he saw the Prime Minister of the United Kingdom. It would be remarkable if the two prime ministers did not discuss the King's association with Mrs. Simpson. There was no other opportunity for personal discussion between Mr. Baldwin and Dominion ministers. Subsequent statements by the various prime ministers give the impression that there was no communication on the subject until 27th November.

Early in October Mrs. Simpson lodged a petition for divorce, which was set down for trial at Ipswich Assizes.

18th October.

The Prime Minister of the United Kingdom asked the King for an interview under conditions of secrecy, naming the subject-matter, and stating that it was urgent.[2]

---

[1] Contrast the view of Mr. John Foster in *The Nineteenth Century*, February 1937, p. 234.

[2] Speech of Mr. Baldwin in the House of Commons on 10th December 1936, 318 *House of Commons Debates*, 5s., 2186–96 (hereinafter cited as 'Speech'), col. 2188.

He informed neither his colleagues in the United Kingdom cabinet nor the Dominions of this step.

20th October.

The interview[1] took place at Fort Belvedere. It appears from Mr. Baldwin's account of it to the House that it took the form of a courteous admonition to the King. His advice was subject to every reserve in a formal sense: that is, he did not profess to be speaking on behalf of his cabinet, or of the Dominions, but only for himself. He spoke, nevertheless, in the character of prime minister, as well as in the character of a friend:[2] no prime minister, whatever his independent personal friendship with a monarch may be, can do otherwise. He did not press for an answer.[3] He spoke without reserve.[4]

He expressed the view that the British monarchy was an immense power for good; that it was by no means invulnerable; that reports of the kind then current were likely, if they continued, to do it damage; and that such damage might be irreparable. He expressed his 'anxiety and desire that such criticism might not have cause to go on'.[5] He referred to the pending divorce proceedings, and to the 'danger' of the 'period of suspense' that might result from the granting of a decree *nisi*.[6]

The King, it seems, said: 'You and I must settle this matter together; I will not have any one interfering.'[7] He also expressed a desire to 'take this action quickly'.[8]

Mr. Baldwin reported his interview to a few of his senior colleagues, but not to the whole Cabinet. Neither he nor the King reported it to the Dominions.

27th October.

At Ipswich Assizes a decree *nisi* was made by Mr. Justice Hawke in the case of *Simpson* v. *Simpson*, which was undefended, after evidence of the usual type.

16th November.

The King sent for Mr. Baldwin (who had already formed the intention of seeking an interview with him) and the second interview took place at

---

[1] Reported in speech, cols. 2188–90.

[2] 'I felt that in the circumstances there was only one man who could speak to him and talk the matter over with him, and that man was the Prime Minister. I felt doubly bound to do it by my duty, as I conceived it, to the country and my duty to him not only as a counsellor but as a friend.' Speech, col. 2188. 'I told him I had come—naturally, I was his Prime Minister—but I wanted to talk it over with him as a friend to see if I could help him in this matter.' Speech, col. 2189.

[3] Speech, col. 2188.

[4] 'There is nothing I have not told His Majesty of which I thought he ought to be aware—nothing.' Speech, col. 2188.

[5] Speech, col. 2189.   [6] Speech, col. 2190.

[7] Speech, col. 2190. Mr. Baldwin narrates these as the King's words.

[8] Speech, col. 2190. The words are Mr. Baldwin's. The context does not show what action is referred to.

Buckingham Palace.[1] Mr. Baldwin spoke first. His advice was again subject to formal reserves, but its substance appears to have been imperative.

Mr. Baldwin spoke first, for fifteen to twenty minutes. The gist of his argument appears from his own account of it to have been: the King must obey the voice of the people in public matters; the identity of the Queen is a public matter; therefore, the King must obey the voice of the people in choosing a Queen. The people would not give its approbation to Mrs. Simpson's being Queen; therefore, the King must not marry her.[2] The King replied, 'I am going to marry Mrs. Simpson and I am prepared to go.' Mr. Baldwin expressed concern, and made no further comment.[3]

25th November.

The King sent for Mr. Baldwin. At the interview he inquired what possibility there was of legislation authorizing a morganatic marriage.[4] Mr. Baldwin refused to give a formal answer, but replied to a further inquiry from the King that his informal reaction was that the United Kingdom parliament would never pass such a bill. He told the King that he could not give a formal answer without first consulting the whole cabinet and the Dominion prime ministers. The King asked that a formal examination of the question on those lines should be made.[5]

27th November.

Mr. Baldwin informed the Dominion prime ministers of the interview of 25th November and presented to them an enumeration of the three possibilities of normal marriage, morganatic marriage, and abdication, with his views thereon. He requested the *personal* opinions of the Prime Ministers, and their assessments of the views of their peoples, on the alternatives.[6] It appears that the request was expressed to be made informally and confidentially.

[1] Speech, col. 2190.　　[2] Speech, cols. 2190-1.

[3] Speech, col. 2191. Mr. Baldwin on 27th November telegraphed an account of this and the preceding interview to dominion prime ministers. Their accounts to their parliaments of the contents of this telegram are second-hand accounts of the interviews. Mr. Lyons, in the Australian House of Representatives on 11th December, reported the telegram as stating 'that His Majesty had stated his intention of marrying Mrs. Simpson, but that at the same time His Majesty had said that he appreciated that the idea of her becoming Queen and her children successors to the Throne was out of the question, and that consequently he contemplated abdicating and leaving the Duke of York to ascend the Throne' (*Sydney Morning Herald*, 12th December). General Hertzog, in the South African House of Assembly on 25th January, said that the telegram informed him 'of a discussion between the King and himself [Mr. Baldwin] on 16th November at which the King informed him of his fixed intention to marry a certain lady, and that he contemplated abdicating in favour of the Duke of York' (*Cape Times*, 26th January).

[4] i.e. a marriage which, while making the lady the King's wife, would not make her Queen.　　[5] Speech, cols. 2191-2.

[6] The request was so described by General Hertzog to the House of Assembly on 25th January. Presumably it was made to the other Dominions in the same form.

On the same day the United Kingdom cabinet met and decided against a morganatic marriage.

28th November–1st December.

Mr. Lyons replied to Mr. Baldwin's message of 27th November that in his view 'the proposed marriage, if it led to Mrs. Simpson becoming Queen, must incur widespread condemnation, and that the alternative proposal, or something in the nature of a specially sanctioned morganatic marriage, would run counter to the best popular conceptions of the Royal Family.'[1]

General Hertzog replied on 30th November that the King should be dissuaded from the marriage; of the alternative evils, abdication was the less. 'The one would be a great shock, but the other would prove a permanent wound.'[2]

Mr. Mackenzie King, on a date not stated, 'advised Premier Baldwin the people of Canada would not approve of marriage to Mrs. Simpson, whether she was to become Queen or not.'[3]

None of these three prime ministers had consulted their cabinets.

The remaining prime ministers, with one lukewarm exception, took a similar line. Whether their cabinets were consulted does not appear.

2nd December.

The King called Mr. Baldwin to a fourth interview and asked for an answer to his question. Mr. Baldwin replied that the inquiries he had thought proper to make were not complete,[4] but that they 'had gone far enough to show that neither the Dominions nor [in the United Kingdom] would there be any prospect of such legislation being accepted'.

Mr. Baldwin, in his narration, goes on to state that the King thereafter regarded the morganatic question as closed, and that thereafter only two alternatives were considered: complete abandonment of the project of marriage, and abdication.[5]

Two English provincial newspapers, taking as their cue or as their pretext a remark by the Bishop of Bradford on the preceding day which had no obvious connexion with the matter, published the news of the King's desire to marry Mrs. Simpson.

3rd December.

The morning press of the whole United Kingdom and all the newspapers of the Empire followed.

[1] Mr. Lyons's speech in the House of Representatives, 11th December (*Sydney Morning Herald*, 12th December).
[2] General Hertzog's speech in the House of Assembly, 25th January (*Cape Times*, 26th January).
[3] In the House of Commons, on 18th January (*Montreal Gazette*, 19th January).
[4] This, presumably, was a reference to the fact that Mr. Baldwin had not yet complied with the King's request that the Dominion prime ministers should be asked to examine the morganatic question *formally*.
[5] Speech, col. 2192.

4th–9th December.

There was public discussion throughout the Empire. The Australian Commonwealth Parliament and the Dáil were summoned; the United Kingdom parliament was already in session. The Canadian, South African, and New Zealand parliaments remained in recess.

On or about 5th December, Mr. Baldwin suggested that Dominion *governments* might like formally to advise the King direct. On 5th December the Australian cabinet,[1] on 6th December the South African cabinet,[2] on 8th December the Canadian cabinet,[3] and on 9th December the United Kingdom cabinet,[4] gave formal advice. This advice in each case asked the King to remain on the Throne, and assumed or stated that he could not remain on the Throne if he should marry Mrs. Simpson. Each of the four governments preferred abdication to marriage of any kind. What advice, if any, the New Zealand government tendered has not been disclosed. The Irish Free State government did not tender any formal advice.[5] Both of these governments, however, at least let it be understood that they had no objection to the actions which were in fact taken by the British government.

10th December.

The King executed an 'instrument of abdication' in the following terms:

'I, Edward VIII, of Great Britain, Ireland, and the British Dominions beyond the Seas, King, Emperor of India, do hereby declare My irrevocable determination to renounce the Throne for Myself and for My descendants, and My desire that effect should be given to this Instrument of Abdication immediately.'

This document was not addressed to any particular person.

In a message to the House of Commons the King announced his decision, reciting the instrument of abdication, and expressed his anxiety 'that there should be no delay of any kind in giving effect to this instrument'.[6] Similar messages were sent to the Dominion parliaments.

Upon the motion that the Message be considered, Mr. Baldwin made the speech from which the foregoing account of events has been principally drawn.

At 6.40 p.m. His Majesty's Declaration of Abdication Bill was brought in to the House of Commons and given a first reading.

On the same day the Canadian Privy Council passed an Order in Council expressing the request and consent of Canada to the Bill.

---

[1] Mr. Lyons in the House of Representatives, 11th December.
[2] General Hertzog in the House of Assembly, 25th January.
[3] Mr. Mackenzie King in the House of Commons, 18th January.
[4] Speech, col. 2195.
[5] Mr. De Valera in Dáil Éireann, 11th December.
[6] 318 *H. C. Deb., 5s.,* 2185–6.

11th December.

Each House of the Australian Commonwealth parliament passed during the day a resolution expressing its assent to the enactment of His Majesty's Declaration of Abdication Act, 1936, by the United Kingdom parliament. Since Canberra time is ten hours in advance of Greenwich time, the resolutions were passed before the House of Commons met.

The House of Commons and the House of Lords passed the Bill through all remaining stages, and it received the Royal assent by Royal Commission in the House of Lords at 1.52 p.m. By its terms it came into force immediately.

The Act[1] recites that—

'the Dominion of Canada pursuant to the provisions of section four of the Statute of Westminster, 1931, has requested and consented to the enactment of this Act, and the Commonwealth of Australia, the Dominion of New Zealand, and the Union of South Africa have assented thereto.'

Section I (1) enacts that the instrument of abdication shall have effect, that Edward VIII shall cease to be King, that there shall be a demise of the Crown, and that 'the member of the Royal Family then next in succession to the Throne shall succeed thereto'. Section I (2) deprives Edward VIII and his descendants of any title to the Throne. Section I (3) frees him and his descendants from the operation of the Royal Marriages Act.

On the same day, Dáil Éireann passed the Constitution (Amendment No. 27) Act, 1937.[2] It eliminates all reference to the King and the Governor-General from the Constitution of the Free State, but authorizes the Executive Council 'to the extent and subject to any conditions which may be determined by law' to avail itself, for the purpose of diplomatic appointments and international agreements, of any organ used for the purposes by the other nations of the British Commonwealth.[3]

12th December.

King George VI was proclaimed in London, Ottawa, Canberra, Pretoria, St. John's, and in many other places throughout the Empire.[4]

Dáil Éireann passed the Executive Authority (External Relations) Act, 1937,[5] and it was signed by the Chairman of the Dáil It provided, first, that:[6]

'It is hereby declared and enacted that, so long as Saorstát Eireann is associated with the following nations, that is to say, Australia, Canada, Great Britain, New Zealand, and South Africa, and so long as the king [*sic*] recognized by those nations as the symbol of their co-operation continues to act on behalf of each of these nations (on the

---

[1] 1 Edw. 8, c. 3. [2] No. 57 of 1936. [3] s. 51, as amended.
[4] The Proclamation appeared in the *New Zealand Gazette* on the same day, but was not read in the Dominion until 14th December.
[5] No. 58 of 1936. [6] s. 3 (1).

advice of the several Governments thereof) for the purposes of the appointment of diplomatic and consular representatives and the conclusion of international agreements, the king so recognized may, and is hereby authorized to, act on behalf of Saorstát Éireann for the like purposes as and when advised by the Executive Council so to do.'

Secondly, it enacted[1] that upon the passing of the Act the Instrument of Abdication should have effect according to its tenor, and that the King should be the person who would, if King Edward had died on 10th December, be his successor under Free State law.

Events in the Dominions during January 1937 (at the end of which month this note went to press) are mentioned in the ensuing comments upon the situation in each Dominion. For most of these events the writer has had to rely on newspaper reports.

LEGAL AND CONSTITUTIONAL POSITION

King Edward VIII

King Edward behaved throughout in accordance with law. An absolute renunciation of the throne might conceivably be regarded as a dereliction of statutory duty; but the Instrument of Abdication was merely a request that he should be relieved of his statutory duties.

His statement to Mr. Baldwin that 'you and I must settle this matter together; I will not have any one interfering', indicates a misapprehension of the constitutional rights of his Dominion advisers, and must therefore be regarded as constitutionally unfortunate.

If, in forming his decision to abdicate, he allowed himself to be influenced by anything the Prime Minister of the United Kingdom said, he acted, in the opinion of the writer, unconstitutionally in not first allowing his Dominion advisers an equal opportunity to influence his decision.[2] If, however, he came to his decision independently of anything he was told by Mr. Baldwin, he broke no convention.

The reflection may be ventured that the present conventional situation places too great a responsibility on the shoulders of an inexperienced monarch, so long as he has, comparatively speaking, no opportunity of intimacy with Dominion advisers.

The United Kingdom

The abdication of King Edward VIII and the succession of King George VI were, so far as the United Kingdom was concerned, in every way regular from the point of view of strict law.

In the opinion of the writer, the convention requiring the assent of Dominion parliaments was sufficiently complied with by the assents subsequently given. The absence from the preamble of His Majesty's Declaration of Abdication Act, 1936, of a recital of the assent of the Irish

---

[1] s. 3 (2).   [2] The view here stated does not command universal assent.

Free State government is immaterial, since no such recital is required by law or convention.

If, when he advised the King informally against marriage with Mrs. Simpson on 16th November, Mr. Baldwin believed that his advice would, or might, affect the decision of the King, either with regard to the marriage or with regard to abdication, he committed, in the opinion of the writer, a breach of convention in so acting without having consulted the Dominion prime ministers beforehand.[1] For such a breach of convention the United Kingdom government was vicariously responsible. If, on the other hand, the King's mind was believed by Mr. Baldwin to be, and was in fact, irrevocably made up on both these issues, so that the advice neither had nor was expected to have any effect, it constituted no breach of convention.

Canada

Section 4 of the Statute of Westminster having been complied with by virtue of the Canadian Order in Council of 10th December and the consequent recital of Canada's request and consent, His Majesty's Declaration of Abdication Act, 1936, validly effected the change of monarch for Canada simultaneously with the United Kingdom.

Upon its meeting in January the Canadian parliament regularized the conventional position by passing an Act expressing its assent to the United Kingdom Act.

Mr. Bennett's criticism,[2] if valid, does not detract from the validity of the succession, but merely places it twenty-four hours earlier. The view of Mr. Woodsworth, leader of the C.C.F. Party,[3] that convention required the assent of the Dominion parliament to precede the enactment of a change in the law of the succession by the United Kingdom, is, in the opinion of the writer, erroneous. Mr. Woodsworth further accused Mr. Mackenzie King of conspiring to force King Edward off the Throne,[4] alleging that Mr. Baldwin put the King in a position which left him no alternative.[5] Mr. King's vindication of Mr. Baldwin, as reported,[6] does not tally with Mr. Baldwin's own account. But as against Mr. King the accusation is merely political; whatever view is taken of Mr. Baldwin's action, Mr. King broke no convention in assenting to it subsequently or in accepting its results.

Canadian action was therefore regular in both law and convention.

---

[1] This view is not accepted by some authorities. See, e.g., Mr. John Foster in *The Nineteenth Century*, loc. cit.

[2] Above, pp. 616, n. 3.

[3] House of Commons, 14th and 15th January (*Montreal Gazette*, 15th and 16th January).

[4] House of Commons, 19th January (*Montreal Gazette*, 20th January).

[5] House of Commons, 15th January (*Winnipeg Free Press*, 16th January).

[6] 'King Edward had first consulted Mr. Baldwin about his proposed marriage, and Mr. Baldwin had given his opinion. He had not placed the King in any position': Mr. King in the House of Commons, 15th January (*Winnipeg Free Press*, 16th January).

Australia

The means by which the succession was effected in Australia are legally and constitutionally impeccable from every point of view.

His Majesty's Declaration of Abdication Act, 1936, applied to Australia *suo proprio vigore*, independently of the Statute of Westminster. The recital therein of Australia's assent was a mere courtesy. The Commonwealth parliament alone of Dominion parliaments complied fully and literally with convention by assenting to the Act before it was passed.

New Zealand

The Act applied to New Zealand *suo proprio vigore*.

At the time of going to press Parliament had not met, but there was no doubt that it would express its assent either by Act, as in Canada, or by resolution, as in Australia.

South Africa

The writer is unable to accept the view of the South African government on the effect of s. 5 of the Status of the Union Act, and its view that unilateral abdication is possible and on this occasion took place. But it is not suggested that these views can by any means be dismissed as perverse. Competent authorities outside South Africa can be found who agree with both of them.

The government's view on abdication is declared by His Majesty King Edward VIII's Declaration of Abdication Bill, and will on that account probably be accepted in South African courts; but the Bill is so drafted that it is unlikely that the question will fall to be decided in litigation.

In the official South African view, the abdication of King Edward and the accession of King George took effect for the whole Empire upon the execution of the Instrument of Abdication on 10th December. The disinheritance of King Edward's possible issue and descendants, however, does not, in this view, take effect for South Africa until the passing of His Majesty King Edward VIII's Abdication Bill.[1]

On the alternative views that the United Kingdom Act effected for South Africa either the whole change or the disinheritance of the possible issue and dependants, the South African Bill will adequately serve the purpose of expressing the assent of the South African parliament within the convention.

On any view, therefore, the succession in South Africa will be legally and conventionally regular.

Irish Free State

It is not appropriate to discuss here the change in the relation of the Crown to the Free State which was brought about by the Irish legislation summarized above. Nor is there room to consider the arguments for the

---

[1] There seemed at the time of going to press no doubt that the Bill would be passed in its then form, and this is here assumed.

various views which are held concerning the dates of the abdication and accession respectively.

The principal possible views are: that the abdication and the accession occurred simultaneously on the passing of the United Kingdom Act on 11th December; that they occurred simultaneously on the passing of the Executive Authority (External Relations) Act on 12th December; that they occurred simultaneously on the execution of the Instrument of Abdication on 10th December; that King Edward abdicated on 10th December, and King George acceded simultaneously, but was removed on 11th December and reinstated on 12th December; that King Edward was removed on 11th December and King George adopted on 12th December. It is also theoretically arguable that King Edward was not at any time validly removed from the throne for the Free State.

The writer does not presume to express a preference among these views. It is, however, likely that, if the Free State Courts had to express a view, they would hold that King Edward was removed by the constitutional amendment of 11th December, and King George adopted by the Act of 12th December.

The Acts of 11th and 12th December, even if they had not purported to create a kingless interregnum of one day, would have been, and are, breaches both of the Irish Treaty and, in the opinion of the writer, of that fundamental convention of the Commonwealth which declares that the members of the Commonwealth are united by a common allegiance to the Crown. It should be added that the present government of the Free State does not regard the Treaty or the conventions of the Commonwealth as binding.

The conventions specifically relating to the law of succession were not, however, infringed. Mr. De Valera, in the Dáil on 11th December, declared that his government was under no obligation to consult other Commonwealth governments before initiating legislation touching the succession to the throne.[1] This was a repudiation of an undoubted convention. But since the effect of the legislation introduced without consultation was, so far as it touched the succession, merely to bring Free State law into line with the alteration proposed by the initiating government, which was the United Kingdom government, consultation could have made no difference. Convention, being a matter of common sense, does not demand otiose acts. No convention, therefore, seems to have been broken.

[1] *Irish Times*, 12th December.

LIST OF CASES CITED

Abbot v. City of St. John, 566 n.[4]

in re Adam 518 n.[7], 520 n.[5, 6].

Advocate General of Bengal v. Ranee Surnomoyee Dossee, 518 n.[1]

Aeronautics Case, 568 n.[4]

Allbright v. Hydro-Electric Power Co., of Ontario, 553 n.[2]

Amalgamated Society of Engineers v. Adelaide S. S. Co., 563 and n.[5], 564, 566 n.[4]

in re Anderson, 519 n.[4]

Armitage v. Armitage, 518 n.[6]

Arnold v. King-Emperor, 554 n.[3]

Attorney-General v. O'Kelly, 560 n.[2]

Attorney-General for Manitoba v. Worthington, 566 n.[4]

Attorney-General for the Commonwealth v. Colonial Sugar Refining Co., 566 and n.[5], 567 and n.[4]

Attorney-General for New South Wales v. Trethowan, 523 n.[4], 525 n.[4], 551 n.[3], 566, 580 n.[6]

Attygalle v. R., 554 n.[3]

Aviation Case, 565 n.[4]

Bank of Toronto v. Lambe, 568 n.[5]

Baxter's Case, 566 n.[4]

Baxter v. Federal Commissioner of Taxation, 566.

Blankard v. Galdy, 514 n.[2], 516 n.[1]

Bonham's Case, 510 n.[4]

British Coal Corporation v. R., 527 n.[2], 549–50, 550 n.[5], 551, 557–60, 564, 568 n.[4], 588, 589, 596, 612 n.[4]

Cahill v. Attorney-General, 523 n., 536 n.[6]

Calvin's Case, 510 n.[1], 514 n.[3], 515 and n.[6], 516 n.[2], 519 n.[1], 520 n.[3].

Cameron v. Kyte, 516 n.[2]

Campbell v. Hall, 515, 516 n.[1, 2], 518

Carolan v. Minister of Defence, 537, 560 n.[2]

Cité de Montreal v. Ecclésiastiques de St. Sulpice, 552 n.[6]

Clayborne's Case, 519 n.[6]

Clergue v. Murray, 552 n.[7]

Craw v. Ramsey, 515 n.[6], 520 n.[7]

Cushing v. Dupuy, 548 n.[5]

Daily Telegraph v. McLaughlin, 552 n.[5]

Deakin v. Webb, 563 n.[2]

D'Emden v. Pedder, 563 n.[2], 564 n.[1]

Donegani v. Donegani, 520 n.[5, 6]

Duncan v. Queensland, 565 n.[5]

Dutton v. Howell, 516 n.[7], 517 n.[1], 520 n.[4]

Edwards v. Attorney-General for Canada, 568 n.[4]

Edwards' Case, 569 n.[1]

Engineers' Case, 563 and n.[5], 564, 566 n.[4]

Flint v. Webb, 565 n.[7]

Fogarty v. Donoghue, 537 n.[1]

Foggitt Jones and Co. v. New South Wales, 565 n.[5]

Forbes v. Cochrane, 516 n.[2]

Gieves, Ltd. v. O'Connor, 539 n.[5]

Great Western Railway v. Mostyn, 555 n.[2]

Hepburn v. Grimswold, 570 n.[1]

Heydon's Case, 562

Hull v. McKenna, 553

James v. Cowan, 567

James v. Commonwealth, 551 n.[3], 564 n.[5], 565 and n.[8], 567

Jephson v. Riera, 516 n.[2]

King v. Victoria Insurance Co., 554 n.[8]

Lautour v. Teesdale, 518 n.[1]

Leen v. President of the Executive Council, 560 n.[2]

Legal Tender Cases, 570 n.[1]

Lindsay v. Oriental Bank, 518

London Finance and Discount Co. v. Butler, 538 n.[9]

Lynam v. Butler, No. 1, 553

Lynam v. Butler, No. 2, 537

McAlister (or Donoghue) v. Stevenson, 545 n.[1]

McArthur's Case, 565 n.[5]

McCawley v. R., 551 n.[3]

Marbury v. Madison, 538

Markwald v. Attorney-General, 520 n.[7]

Moore's Case (see below)